The Strangest Town in Alaska

The History of Whittier, Alaska
and the Portage Valley

Text, Illustrations and
Photographs by
Alan Taylor

Additional Photography by
Christina Taylor

Kokogiak Media

The Strangest Town in Alaska
The History of Whittier, Alaska and the Portage Valley

Copyright © 2000 Kokogiak Media

All rights reserved. No part of this book may be used or reproduced in any form or by any means, electronic or mechanical, including photocopying, recording, or by any information storage or retrieval system, without prior written permission of the publisher.

Manufactured in the United States of America
by McNaughton & Gunn, Inc., Saline, MI

ISBN 0-9677860-0-2
Library of Congress Control Number: 00-131104

Published by:

Kokogiak Media
9457 Phinney Ave N
Seattle, WA 98103

Website: **http://www.kokogiak.com**
Email: **info@kokogiak.com**

Photo Credits:

Unless specifically noted below, photographs in this book are property of and Copyright © 2000 Kokogiak Media.

Anchorage Museum of History and Art:
Photos on pages 20, 30, 38, 39, 40, 44, 45, 46, 47, 48, 50, 51, 52 (both), 53, 54, 55, 56, 57, 58, 59, 72, 79, 104 (upper), and Chapters 3, 4, & 6 title pages.

Steinbrugge Collection, Earthquake Engineering Research Center, University of California, Berkeley:
Photos on pages 67 (lower), 77, 78, 80, 81, 82, 83, C-1 (bottom), C-2 (upper right)

U.S. Library of Congress:
Photos on pages 9, 68, 69, 70 (all), 71 (both)

Hope and Sunrise Historical Society:
Photos on page 21, and Chapter 2 title page

Acknowledgements

No book is created in a vacuum, and this labor of love has benefited greatly from the assistance of many others. I'd like to thank my wife and partner, Christina for her help, support, and assistance — and her objective eye.

I'd also like to extend my gratitude to the people of Whittier, Hope and Girdwood, Alaska. Specifically, thanks to Kay Shepard for her time and insights about life in Whittier, and to Brad Phillips for helping me work the bugs out of my early drafts. Also, a big thank you to David Kasser and Lynne Glatz for their gracious support and hospitality.

The following people and organizations also contributed to the completion of this work, and I'd like to extend my thanks (in no particular order) to Diane Brenner and the staff of the Anchorage Museum of History and Art, Pete & Marilyn Heddell and the Whittier Chamber of Commerce, Kent Sturgis of Epicenter Press, Karen Shaak, Sergey Avtandilov, Shane Luitjens, the staff of the Loussac Library, Ann and Billy Miller of the Hope and Sunrise Historical Society, the Whittier Museum, the Whittier Library, the Seattle Public Library, the University of Washington Special Collections staff, the Governor's office of the State of Alaska, Tom Dougherty and the Alaska Department of Transportation, and Gray Line of Alaska — for starting me down this journey years ago.

*Dedicated to Christina.
My love and gratitude
know no bounds.*

Foreword

After spending several years in Alaska, I find myself thinking about the Great Land often. I have moved back south now, and like many others who have gone "outside," I find myself wondering if moving was the right choice. When asked about Alaska, I can only respond with words of praise, fondly remembering days and nights up North.

For a couple of winters I had a job that entailed driving around the lower 48 states promoting tourism to Alaska, and answering questions from Tallahassee to Las Vegas. One question that I heard often was "which is your favorite place in Alaska?" The first few times I just said "I don't know," and went on about how every place is lovely up there. But, as time went by, I found that one place kept coming to mind when I was asked — Portage Valley and Whittier.

The immediate follow-up question is "why?" Well, because it's beautiful and strange — attractive and incongruous — a lot like Alaska. Whittier is a unique Alaskan town, far from typical, and Portage Valley is a standout feature among mountainous beauty. Geographically, anthropologically and historically, this region stands out.

Portage Glacier has grown to become the most-visited tourist destination in Alaska, over 700,000 visitors every year. Nearby Price William Sound is world-famous (or infamous) due in part to the 1989 oil spill. Yet Whittier, a port on Prince William Sound, and less than 5 miles from Portage Glacier, remains shadowed in relative obscurity — a curious footnote in Alaskan history.

I found the area more and more interesting and spent some time researching its background. Unfortunately, not much could be found in the way of records or articles. So, a curiosity formed that grew into this book.

I hope that you, the reader, will have already visited or will soon be going to visit Portage and Whittier, as well as the rest of Alaska, to experience these places in person. No matter how much detail or character is put into a written history, it pales compared to the experience of "really going there."

— Alan Taylor

Introduction

The Small Alaskan Town as an archetype seems fairly well defined by popular myth and cultural reference — "Northern Exposure" being the most recent and powerful definer. Small Alaskan towns are anything but typical — often they are more bizarre than any Hollywood writer could dream up. Whittier is such a town. Imagine a place in late-20th century America that is accessible only by boat or train — a town with a tiny population that once claimed the largest building in Alaska. If Alaska is where Americans go to "get away from it all," then Whittier is one of the places *Alaskans* go to "get away from it all."

Whittier is weird, it is just flat-out strange. It is also gorgeous — secluded and wild. That blend has drawn people to explore or to live there for the past five decades. Visitors today find a community that is the result of years of political conflict, dreams of peaceful solitude, aborted ambitions and abandoned plans. The town is better known as a way-station than a destination. It is the gateway to Prince William Sound for Anchorage — the most populated region in Alaska. Whittier's own population of around 300 people lives tucked away in a few areas of a massive military complex that was once suited to house up to 30,000 people.

Inaccessible, stark, windblown and wet, Whittier sits in one of the most inhospitable areas of South Central Alaska. An annual precipitation of nearly 175 inches drenches the hillsides and continually builds the nearby glaciers.

Until the year 2000, there were only two ways to reach Whittier — by boat or by train. Though Whittier lies only five miles away from popular Portage Glacier, there was never any road access. The railroad to Whittier traveled only 12 miles — from a remote station on the side of a highway. But these 12 miles included several bridges and two tunnels — one of which runs nearly three miles through the base of a mountain. Now residents and visitors have a new road to use, but what a road — at a cost of $80 million this toll road is a unique system, allowing cars, trucks, buses and trains to alternately share a 2.6 mile long alternating direction, one-lane, shared-use tunnel.

Remoteness and inaccessibility were assets to the U.S. Military - the first entity to build in the region, and by the early 1950s, the military's plans for Whittier became nothing less than grand. One of a complex of buildings, Whittier's Buckner Building is comparable to a land-based aircraft carrier. Nearly as big as a battleship, the structure was created to be a self-sufficient, "city under one roof." It ended up becoming the largest building in Alaska — in the smallest and newest town. But the military has its whims — as history has shown — and the entire town of Whittier was soon mothballed as surplus, only to rise from its ashes as a modern town.

The following is an exploration of the history of Passage Canal, the surrounding lands and people and its contemporary existence. Much of the Whittier's past is recent — it is barely more than 50 years old as a city — but the region has been active and interesting for centuries.

Table of Contents

Foreword   i
Introduction   iii

Chapter I -- From Icy Beginnings to a Hot Property.. 1
    Brand new lands
    Emissaries from Tsar Peter
    First documented use of Portage Pass
    The British arrive -- and Turn Again
    Spain arrives late in the game
    The return of the Britons
    Whidbey seeks out the pass
    The RAK moves south -- and loses its grip
    The collapse of Russia (in America)
    The U.S. gains interest in the North

Chapter II -- America's Newest Possession, A Golden End to the 19th Century............ 15
    Russian America becomes U.S. property
    Ivan Petroff, Counting heads and making enemies
    Hints of Alaska's golden future
    Gold Fever -- Early stage symptoms
    Sunrise -- Turnagain's first community
    Frontier government in its infancy
    "The Bulldog" sails north
    The Big Strike happens quietly
    The Sun begins to set in Sunrise
    Charles Blackstone and the breakup of '97
    Fearsome weather and the Turnagain Jet
    The Rush is triggered
    "Grab yer gear and head north!"
    An early shadow of Whittier
    Finding the lay of the land
    An expedition across Portage Pass
    "Hurrah for the HAE!"
    A Surprising find

Chapter III -- Mapping, Planning and Building - Alaska becomes a Territory.............. 37
    Alaska becomes a Territory, and a home
    Railroad companies look northward
    A first look at a future port
    Rails reach the Interior
    A look at Southcentral Alaska

Chapter IV -- An Explosion of Development, WWII shapes Alaska.............................. 43
    Reevaluations and announcements
    Early construction begins
    The new rail raises tempers
    A bay by any other name
    Whittier emerges
    "Ever heard of this place?"
    U.S. enters the War
    Japan attacks Alaska
    Whittier is electrified
    Completions
    Activation and Inauguration
    Ending a year of Japanese occupation
    Preparing for Kiska
    Whittier -- the newest cog in the War Machine
    Conclusions

Chapter V -- From Massive Plans to Meager Ends.. 63
    Planning a future Whittier -- on a Grand Scale
    "A city under one roof"
    Southcentral Alaska grows into the 1950's
    Whittier's "other" monolithic structure
    Whittier reaches its high point
    Statehood, and Whittier's fast fade
    Mothballed
    Unceremonious closure

Chapter VI -- The Quake, and the Slow Road to Recovery... 77
    "Just when it looked like it couldn't get worse..."
    The morning after
    Submarine landslides
    Getting back to business
    Whittier regains a population
    Whittier becomes a city
    Residents liked the town so much...they bought it
    Growth in the 1980's
    Mixed tragedy on Good Friday
    Boatloads of tourists

Chapter VII -- Whittier Now... 97
    The Road
    Whittier today
    Life in isolation
    Bring on the cable TV
    Activity in Passage Canal
    "Why would you want to live there?"
    Rumors abound
    Entering the 21st Century

Chapter I
From Icy Beginnings to a Hot Property

Brand new lands

To gain an appreciation of how geographically young and remote the area around Whittier is, consider that when Christopher Columbus landed in America, the entire fjord of Passage Canal lay under several miles of glacial ice. Years of grinding and digging by Mother Nature created the features that would determine man's role in the area.

From 1400-1500 AD, global warming had ended the recent Ice Age and crawled north, past the 60th parallel. Glacial ice melted at accelerated rates, retreating into the mountains. A group of people living on the shorelines of present-day South Central Alaska called themselves Chugachigmiut, or Chugach (chew-gatch) The Chugach were Native Americans called Inuit (inn-you-it), and were adapted to their climate, living off the richness of life present wherever the land meets the sea. They were intimately familiar with the seaways, coves, islands and glaciers forming their home. Glacial change is slow enough to be measured in generations, and the Chugach of the Lower Kenai area traded stories for years of fantastic glacial retreat, exchanging tales of new islands and fjords emerging with the passing of every year.

Over several hundred years, the mass of ice covering Prince William Sound retreated back up into surrounding mountainsides and valleys, unveiling 200 square miles of sea and land. The massive weight of the ice pack — in places miles thick — pressed on the land for years, smashing it tight. Like grass on a lawn that springs up after being flattened, small islands poked up above sea level for years after being uncovered. High mountains once appeared as islands of stone above a high sea of ice, called Nunataks (noon-a-taks). These once solitary Nunataks, now unsheathed mountains, lorded over the group of hills, islands and seaways that became known as Prince William Sound.

The Chugach people followed this retreat, staying close to their main source of food and clothing, Harbor Seals. Harbor Seals stay close to glacial faces — where the ice meets the sea — and use the dense pack of icebergs to rest and hide from predatory killer whales. Following the seals, the Chugach settled into many parts of Prince William Sound for the first time. The last time this land was uncovered by ice, hundreds of years before, no humans lived within thousands of miles. The Chugach thrived, finding what many others would come to discover, that Prince William Sound is a treasure of abundance.

Emissaries from Tsar Peter

By the 1700's, generations of Chugach had called Prince William Sound home. Some had heard whispers from trades with neighboring tribes to the south, whispers about strange men with hairy faces, sailing in huge wooden kayaks. It wasn't until 1741 that any of these strangers were seen around this part of South Central Alaska.

The famous Danish sailor Vitus Bering and Russian Alexei Chirikof sailed from Russia's Kamchatka Peninsula in 1741 for their first encounter with the New World. Originally ordered to explore in 1725 by Tsar Peter the Great, the overland trip from Moscow and two previous failed attempts had taken a difficult 16 years. Two ships were launched, Bering commanded the St. Peter, Chirikof had the St. Paul.

In December 1741, shortly after sailing south of Kodiak Island, Bering died aboard ship, suffering from scurvy. Chirikof successfully made it along the coastline as far south as present-day Sitka. The Russians met amicably with curious natives and amassed huge amounts of soft, thick Bobri Morski (Sea Otter) pelts. The Bobri Morski pelts were highly prized in China and Europe, and fetched a high price. Upon Chirikof's return to Moscow, and his reports of abundant furs, the Promyshleniki (explorers, or voyageurs) of Russia began a full charge to this new land, known as Alyeska, or Russian America.

The term "Alyeska" (or variously "Alaqshaq", "Alashka", or "Alaska") is derivative of a Native Aleut term for great mountains — in their poetic language it translates as "where the sea breaks its back." It showed the Aleuts' awe for the great land to the east, beyond their more easily comprehended island existence.

The following years, the Chugach and their neighbors (and sometime enemies) to the west, the Tanaina (Da-nay-na) became very familiar with these Promyshlenikis. Enthusiastic Russians flocked to Siberia, bound for Alyeska, often meeting disastrous ends. Being mainly land dwellers, they were often unfamiliar with open sea sailing, and were unprepared for the fearfully turbulent North Pacific waters. Many sailors died at sea, the ones who made it through found the going rough at best.

Some of the smarter promyshlenikis found that the flexible light two-man Kayaks used by the natives were much more effective for getting around short distances. The Russians called the kayaks "baidarkas", and the Promyshleniki adopted them readily throughout southern Alyeska, as a means for transport and hunting. They even developed a hybrid 3-passenger baidarka — one for a Russian and two for native paddlers.

Thousands of miles from home, living off the land in a difficult northern climate, newcomers quickly abandoned any grand ideas of becoming wealthy, or achieving any success as an individual. The Promyshlenikis learned to cooperate and exploit, impressing and intimidating the natives into hunting for them, offering trades of favors, food, liquor and salvation through the Russian Orthodox Church. Word spread and the natives became interested in what the Russians could offer. Further supplies and funding from Moscow would be needed to maintain this method of business.

In 1789 Gregor Shelikof, businessman and active fur trader in Russian America, was awarded a State Charter by the Tsar, and he founded the Rossiisko-Amerikanskoi Kompanii, (RAK), better known to Americans as the Russian America Company. Alexander Baronof soon became the head of the new company. With imperial backing and a (relatively) steady rate of supplies, the full-scale skinning of Alaska commenced.

Baranof was widely known for his stormy temper, but was known to Kodiak natives as their "little father" who took care of those near him. Based on Kodiak Island, the RAK brought in otter pelts from Tlingits to the east, Aleuts to the west and the Tanaina and Chugach nearby. Sea routes and overland trails that were lightly used before for intertribal trade or warfare became highways of a burgeoning commerce. The Russian traders and company representatives mapped many of them out, furthering their claims of territorial ownership, and strengthening the bonds with the natives, so crucial to the survival of the Promyshlenikis.

The innumerable fjords and bays of Prince William Sound teemed with life, filled with schools of salmon and rafts of Bobri Morski. The Chugach, skilled hunters, circled them, waiting for the otters to dive, anticipating where they would bob back up again for air, and speared them from their kayaks.

Russian attempts to hunt ended miserably, as did those of the Americans and British who followed, due to their use of rifles. Curious otters made easy enough targets, as they allowed close approach of any quiet vessels. However, one shot from a rifle not only killed the otter, but sent its body sinking to the sea floor.

Estimates throughout the many years of otter trade show that rifle hunters recovered only one out of every nine otters shot. The other eight sank away.

First documented use of Portage Pass

The adept Chugach brought their captured pelts to nearby Russian trading posts, or to distant Kodiak. One of the main routes of travel from Prince William Sound to points west was made over the isthmus now known as Portage Valley.

Looking at the map of southcentral Alaska on the next page, one sees that Kodiak Island and the Kenai Peninsula are shaped much the same, and were formed similarly as well. The Kenai Peninsula is very nearly an island as well. Over 16,000 square miles of peninsula is joined to the mainland of Alaska by a narrow neck, an isthmus only 15 miles wide, and at its tallest, only 700 feet above sea level.

This isthmus is bordered on the west by Turnagain Arm, the southern branch of Cook Inlet, on the east by Passage Canal, a fjord of western Prince William Sound. The heavy glaciation that carved out most of the valleys, and dug out the basins for the fjords and canals stopped just short of

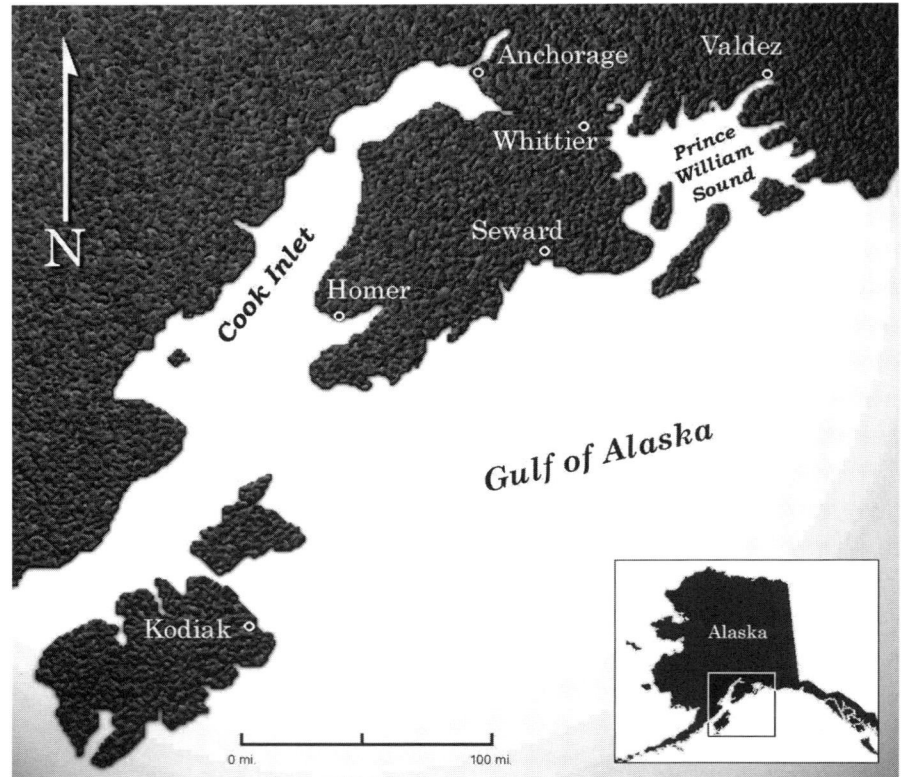

Southcentral Alaska is currently the most populous region in the state of Alaska. Before the Russians arrived, this region was well populated by natives. The Chugach lived in Prince William Sound, and along the south shore of the Kenai Peninsula, (top center of map) and also on Kodiak Island. Their neighbors (and competitors) were the Tanaina, who lived to the north and all along the shores of Cook Inlet. The Chugach and Tanaina spoke entirely different languages (Alutiiq and Athapaskan, respectively).

making the Kenai an island, and created a natural bottleneck that has been used as a pathway by men for hundreds of years.

The Chugach might hunt all day or for several days, camp out on the western shore of Passage Canal, and climb over land and glacier, portaging to Turnagain Arm, there to kayak down to Russian trading posts. "Portage" was a term popularized by the French-Canadian Voyageurs of North America and spread into common usage throughout the west. It means to carry oneself or materials from waterway to waterway across a patch of land.

The portage was made by a half mile walk from Passage Canal, a short steep climb to 700 feet, a traverse to Portage Glacier, a treacherous three-mile icy hike to the foot of the glacier and an 11-mile hike (or float, if Portage Creek was unfrozen) to the salt water of Turnagain Arm. The trip was best made in the early spring or late winter months, when the dangerous crevasses were frozen and snow-filled. Summer trips were possible, but risky and rarely attempted.

The British arrive — and Turn Again

In contrast to the Russian sailors, who were just getting their bearings as seafarers, a group of historically accomplished sailors began searching this area, reaching into Russian America first in 1778. Captain James Cook of the H.M.S. Resolution, sailing from the Sandwich Islands (Hawaii), landed first on the coastline of present British Columbia that year. He sailed along the coast as far north as the Arctic Ocean, stopping along the way, making rudimentary maps and searching for any possible paths to a fabled Northwest Passage.

In early summer he briefly explored and named Prince William Sound. He sailed west, and discovered what looked to be a very promising wide inlet heading west-northwest. That bay later took his name, as Cook Inlet. Exploring the inlet further west, Cook anchored the Resolution not far from Fire Island, near what is today Anchorage. He sent men in smaller boats to explore further up the inlet, to determine the nature of the water, whether it was a river or a passage of seawater.

The inlet became increasingly shallow, though the men were miles from any visible ending of the waters. Soon, only a small navigable channel of deep water remained, despite shallower water that spread out for miles around. The channel twisted and curved tortuously, as can be seen in the photograph below, forcing the boats not only to navigate side to side across the inlet, but to go upstream and downstream to stay in deep enough waters. Upon their return and description of the winding waterway, Cook's cartographer marked the place "River Turnagain." The Russians later called it "Vozvrashchenie", meaning "Return Bay".

A view of Turnagain Arm from Mt. Alyeska, above the Girdwood valley. The twisting channels of seawater can be seen during this low tide. The curves and doglegs made finding navigable channels very difficult for early explorers, and led Cook's cartographer to label it "River Turnagain."

Cook enjoyed high esteem in Britain for previous exploratory accomplishments and for excellence at sea as an officer of the Royal Navy. Military decorum at the time was disciplinary and harsh. Not long after this sailing, a fellow officer who was with Cook in Alaska gained infamy for an incident in the south seas. His name was Captain Bligh His loss of command to a mutinous crew in the south Pacific became the stuff of legends, stories and movies as the Mutiny on the Bounty.

Cook, though not considered as cruel as Bligh, was still a taskmaster, and used harsh tactics not only on crew, but on unruly natives wherever he might be. These tactics proved to be his undoing. On the Big Island of Hawaii, just after his 1778 Alaska journey, Cook's men discovered the theft of a small boat while at anchor. Cook, in order to get the boat back, went ashore to make a hostage of some man of importance, a chief or a king. This was a common practice for the Royal Navy, though no less shocking to the natives. Thousands of Hawaiian Islanders surrounded Cook's kidnap party on a beach of Kealakekua Bay. Anger and confusion drove the crowd. Cook ordered the men into the boats. A shot was fired, by whom is unknown. A native man fell dead. The mob pounced on Cook as he ran through the surf for the boats, and clubbed him to death. Later the islanders showed remorse for their actions, but still harbored resentment for the foreigners. It wasn't until 1820 that Western influence gained dominance in Hawaii.

Spain arrives late in the game

In 1790 the Spanish became the third group of European explorers to travel Alaskan waters, after Russia and Britain. Don Salvador Fidalgo failed in several earlier attempts to sail north of Spanish territories near Mexico. He achieved success in mid-1790, and made a short and laborious journey, surveying North American coasts as far north as Prince William Sound. He bestowed place names from Washington State to Alaska that remain to this day (Fidalgo Head, Strait of Juan de Fuca, Revillagigedo Island, etc.) Valdez arm of Prince William Sound was named after a sponsoring Spanish finance minister. A smattering of names remains as the sum of Spanish impact on this region. Troubles in their southern colonies and competition in the north kept them out of it.

Soon the British, Russians and the increasingly active Americans would decide who owned and ruled these lands, giving little or no interest to the established native dwellers.

The return of the Britons

By the arrival of English explorer Captain George Vancouver in South Central Alaska in 1794, Shelikof, Baranof and members of the Russian America Company had celebrated 10 years in an established European colony town on Kodiak Island, their fur trade booming. Vancouver, aboard the H.M.S. Discovery sailed up Cook Inlet in Cook's footsteps. Arriving at the end of navigable waters, Vancouver sent out men under the watch of an officer named Whidbey to explore the "River Turnagain", to determine if it was indeed a river, not just a shallow passage, and if it was a river, to find what lay at its headwaters.

While Whidbey and party explored, a few Russian trappers who traded nearby paddled up to the Discovery. Vancouver, notified of the approach, allowed them on board. They met each other amicably, though communications proved difficult, as neither spoke the others language well. Vancouver asked about the surrounding territory, and the trappers described the wide Matanuska Valley to the north. They confirmed the ending of Turnagain Arm to the east, and at its end, wrote Vancouver, spoke of "a hill or mountain that occupied the space of 15 or 16 verst (12 miles), and that they had there descended into an arm of the sea that had communication with Prince William's Sound; across which isthmus is the route by which they stated that all their intercourse between the Russian settlements in this and that extensive inlet, was now carried on."

The Russians also appeared adamant about ownership. They claimed vehemently that the northern part of North America and all of its islands were property of the Russian Empire, and subject to the Tsar. The Russian trappers left the H.M.S. Discovery peacefully and headed east, toward the end of Turnagain Arm.

Bore Tide

A phenomenon called a **tidal bore**, or "bore tide", occurs when incoming water from a high tide overpowers an outgoing low tide. In a long narrow estuary like Turnagain Arm, the water takes so long to be affected by the tides in the open sea that there is some overlap.

The momentum of water flowing out to sea clashes with the swelling waters of the high tide coming in. High tide waters push forth and actually spill over in a long curving wave stretching from one shore to the other. This wave can be several inches to several feet high.

Whidbey returned, finding that salinity tests and tidal effects proved Turnagain was definitely not a river. Later exploration showed it to be a remarkable body of seawater. Filled almost entirely with silt through its length, the arm at low tide resembles a muddy plain with a single zigzag of a stream gouging the middle. At high tide the opaque, silty seawater covers the mud and looks deceptively like a deep navigable bay between 1 and 3 miles across. Tidal variation is more than 30 feet, second only to the Bay of Fundy in Eastern Canada.

Whidbey seeks out the pass

Sailing away from the dangerous mudflats, Vancouver entered Prince William Sound, arriving in June, 1794. He sent Whidbey out again to explore the western reaches of the sound, another member of the crew named Johnstone sailed to the

Portage Pass, as seen from the end of Whittier's gravel Air Strip. Rising only 700 ft. above sea level, the pass is the lowest point between the Chugach Mountains to the north, and the Kenai Range to the south. The large notch in the pass (visible on the left side) looks inviting, but ends in waterfalls and steep cliff faces. The actual trail can just be seen snaking up the pass in the center right of the photograph, along the bottom of Mt. Maynard. Portage Glacier and Portage Lake lie just on the other side of the pass, less than two miles away.

east. Whidbey and his small team explored several inlets, including present-day Blackstone Bay, Shotgun Cove and Passage Canal. Reaching the head of the yet-to-be-named Passage Canal, he disembarked and sought a possible trail on foot, reporting to Vancouver that "here they had approached within 12 miles of the spot where he had ended his examination of Turnagain Arm. The intermediate space was the isthmus so frequently alluded to before, on either side of which the country was composed of what appeared to him to be lofty, barren, impassable mountains, enveloped in perpetual snow; but the isthmus itself was a valley of some breadth, which though it contained elevated land, was very free from snow, and appeared to be perfectly easy of access."

Meanwhile on the opposite side of Prince William Sound, Johnstone and party made contact with a group of Russian traders. While he stayed with them, he saw a party of Natives delivering skins, and understood that the Natives had made the overland portage from Cook Inlet, canoes skins and all, to Prince William Sound via Whidbey's isthmus. Vancouver himself soon met the same Russian he had spoken with earlier, while anchored in Cook Inlet, and was informed of his crossing of the portage.

Though Whidbey had landed and attempted to find a way over the pass, he never located the trailhead, and returned to the Discovery disappointed, stating that the valley surface looked "tolerably even", and that traversing it should have been easy.

As seen in the photograph on this page, the pass is deceptive approaching from Passage Canal. It is broad and rocky, with a large notch on the left (south) side. On first glance, from sea level, the notch appears to be the natural pathway, but it ends in impassable cliffs and waterfalls. The actual trail begins a half mile to the right (north,) along the side of Mt. Maynard. Much of the level land between the airstrip and the pass is now privately owned. Part of that has been recently sold to the State for use as a staging area for the new tunnel.

Vancouver and his crew returned to England shortly after their visit to Prince William Sound, bringing home much desired detailed maps and charts of the Northwest and leaving behind place names that remain to this day.

The RAK moves south — and loses its grip

In 1799, Alexander Baranof, now completely the recognized head of the Russian America Company, departed Kodiak Island for a more central location in Sitka - hundreds of miles southwest, along the Alaskan coast. (The dire shortage of overhunted otters acted as a driving force in the move.) Not only did Baranof sail, but the entire village of Kodiak went along too. Two tiny Russian ships, the Olga and Konstantin (each only 35 feet long) led more than 300 baidarkas carrying 600 Aleuts on this strange and dangerous exodus. They arrived without major incident weeks later in the island country of southeast Alaska, and founded New Archangel, now known as Sitka.

With Kodiak abandoned, the Russian settlement of Port Etches in Prince William Sound became the prominent Russian America Company presence in Southcentral Alaska. The Tanainas to the west increased their usage of Portage Pass to reach Port Etches after this time. Russian reports of the time tell of a trading post located at the head of Passage Canal, on the site of Whittier's airstrip today. The trading post existed seasonally, with the posted traders returning to Port Etches or New Archangel as the pass became unusable in summer.

An 1849 map of Prince William Sound and Turnagain Arm created by the Russian Navy as part of a wide-reaching survey of their holdings in North America, 18 years before it was all sold to the United States.

The legend reads "MAP, Chugatskoii Bay, prepared by the Colonial Navy, New Archangel, 1849".

Turnagain Arm can be seen at far left - with a still-undefined eastern shore.

From Icy Beginnings to a Hot Property

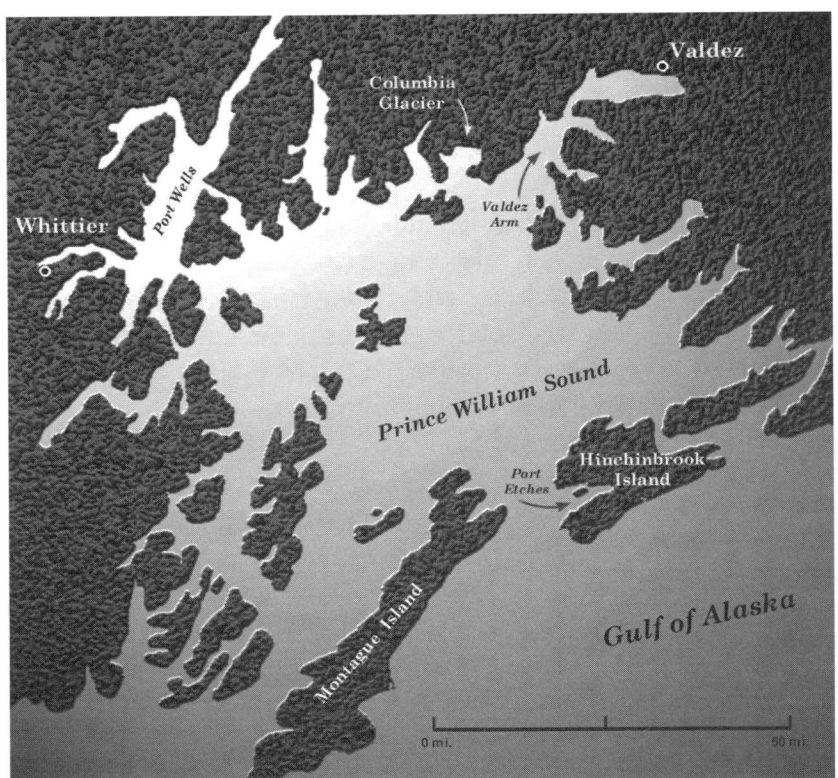

Prince William Sound, framed by Valdez on the northeast corner, and Whittier on on the west. Cruise ships, day boats, fishing vessels, and — infamously — oil tankers all currently share these waterways.

While the Russians had only a small presence on Hinchinbrook Island, at Port Etches in the early 1800's, their influence was felt throughout South Central Alaska.

The natives they had worked with on Kodiak Island were part of the same ethnic group that lived in Prince William Sound (the Chugach), and they traded amongst themselves and with the Tanaina to the northwest.

For the next 30 years, Russian fur trade slowly declined. The Aleuts slowly acclimated to their southern village, and the Russians did their best to maintain New Archangel amongst hostile native neighbors called the Kolosh. The Bobri Morski pelts, once numbering in the tens of thousands, were nearly gone, the sea otters hunted to a mere handful. Trading posts, difficult to maintain, defend and fund, increasingly were abandoned. At this time, furs were in high demand by the corporate and political shareholders in Russia. Under pressure to produce more, Baranof sent hunting parties as far east as the Pribilof Islands and as far south as Baja California, thousands of miles distant.

The American and British presence throughout Alaska grew stronger every day. Britain held claim to much of what would become Canada, The U.S. expanded westward through the early 1800s. These newcomers to Alaska carried on trade with any of its inhabitants, even the Kolosh, enemies of the Russian Settlers. Trades of rifles and gunpowder became frequent, arming many of the angered tribes. Confrontations increased in frequency and violence. Mother Russia began to lose her grip.

After previous attempts to step down, Alexander Baranof finally gave up control of the Russian America Company (RAK) in 1818. He sent word to Moscow earlier for a younger replacement, but miscommunications and a shipwreck prevented any from arriving. Baranof received word that a replacement was due soon, and walked away from both the position with the RAK and the Governorship of New Archangel. Soon after, he set sail for Russia, looking forward to returning after a 28 year absence. Baranof never again saw a Russian hillside. He developed a fever at sea and died quickly. After 28 years of hardship in the frigid north, ironically, Baranof was buried at sea in the warm waters of the Indian Ocean.

The collapse of Russia (in America)

The RAK held on, remaining lucrative for distant stockholders at ever-increasing expense to those living throughout Russian America from Kodiak to New Archangel. To keep profits from fading, managers of the RAK began diversifying, starting fishing operations and sending explorers out in search of minerals. Resident Russian Americans felt their claims to American territory slipping due to diplomatic dealings outside of their control. In 1825 agreements were reached between the U.S., England and Russia to officially limit Russian America's southern border to 54 degrees 40 minutes north latitude, where Alaska's border still terminates. Limits on inland expansion were left open, as the massive Coastal range of mountains made movement to the interior impossible.

Instability in the Russian homeland, primarily Moscow eventually doomed Russian America. Tsar Alexander I became powerful and increasingly reactionary following the end of the Napoleonic Wars. He forbade any political dissent, creating silenced angry masses. Tsar Alexander I died in 1825, passing the torch to Tsar Nicholas who ruled with equal repressiveness. The sparks of revolution started glowing. By the 1860's, the next Tsar, Alexander II had emancipated the Russian serfs, but set them free into a hostile world of poverty and unemployment. A Polish rebellion began and was cruelly stifled by Alexander II. Apprehension and uncertainty gripped Russia's ruling class.

At this same time, advisors and ambassadors returning from Russian America told tales of massive foreign interest and involvement in Russia's North American holdings. Minerals had been discovered — gold, coal and copper — in massive amounts. But the RAK could barely afford to feed its people, and Russia could send no more men nor money to develop or govern the extraction of these minerals. If word of large strikes had leaked out to the world, as it surely would, Russian ministers felt that they could not manage the rush of mostly foreign prospectors. By 1863, Russian domestic concerns so overshadowed Russian America, Moscow virtually abandoned its northwestern colony, leaving New Archangel, (now Sitka) and nearly 600 Russian citizens in an independent limbo.

The U.S. gains interest in the North

Two years later, in 1865, American

William H. Dall led a survey team through the interior of Alaska to map a line for Western Union Telegraph. Western Union was intent on laying cable overland from the Oregon Territory through British Columbia, the Yukon, and Alaska - crossing the Bering Strait to Russia and Europe. Despite the scramble to be the first to link Europe to the U.S., the folks at Western Union sighed a breath of relief a few years later when they lost, and the first successful link was made to Europe via the Trans-Atlantic Cable. Though the Western Union Siberian telegraph line would have been a historic achievement, it would have cost millions, and the remoteness would have made it impossible to maintain.

Western Union scrubbed its telegraph plans, but Dall's surveys did not go unnoticed by others. His reports caught the eye of expansion-minded Washington D.C. With the Civil War just concluded, every politician's mind leaned towards reconstruction and national expansion. Government representatives traveled north to determine the positions of the Russians and British.

Tsar Alexander II sent an emissary named Baron Edward de Stoeckl east to meet with these American newcomers. Baron de Stoeckl laid out nearly $200,000 of his own fortune ($2 million in 1996 dollars) to brighten up Sitka. After preparations were made and all expected guests had arrived, he escorted tours around the area, wined and dined, and made a marvelous sales pitch to the Americans.

Based on reports returned to him, U.S. Secretary of State William H. Seward offered and purchased Alaska outright on March 30th, 1867. The purchase price was $7,200,000 or 2.5 cents an acre — seven million to the Tsar, and two hundred thousand to de Stoeckl to replenish his fortunes. Congress later approved the funding, with reservations, referring to its latest acquisition as "(President) Johnson's Polar Bear Garden", or "Walrussia." It took Alaska years to shake the image of a "frozen wasteland."

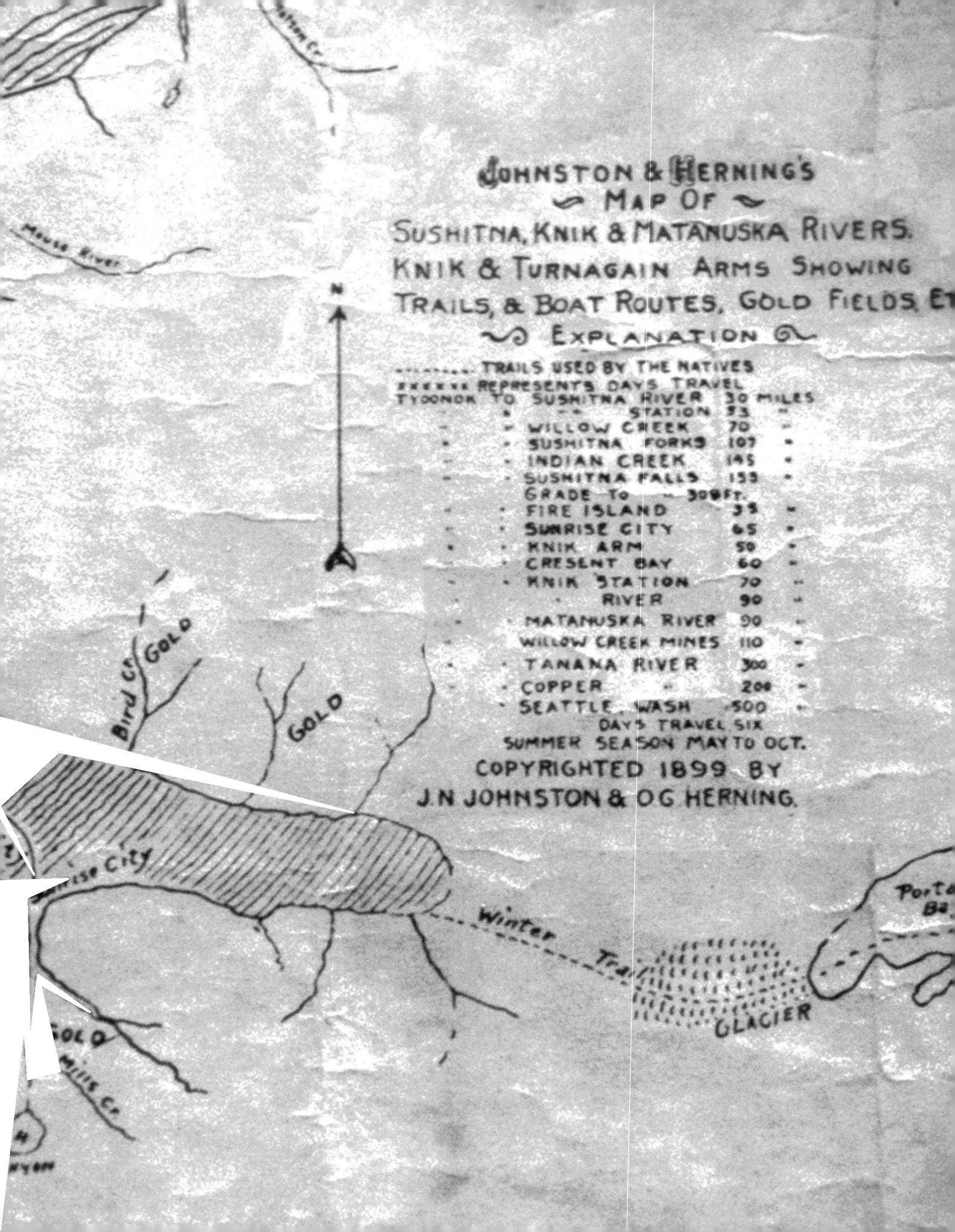

Chapter II
America's Newest Possession and a Golden End to the 19th Century

Russian America becomes U.S. property

Sitka acted as the stage for a sorrowful scene October 18th, 1867. The USS Ossipee steamed in to join the USS John Stephens in Sitka Harbor. 200 American troops drew up and faced another 100 Russian soldiers as the Russian flag was taken down — replaced with a U.S. set of stars and stripes. Overnight the home of nearly a thousand Russian Americans became American land. Most of the newly exiled residents of Sitka decided to return to Russia, though many of them had never seen it. By 1867, a healthy third generation of Russian Americans had been born. The move to a foreign 'Mother' country would prove a difficult one. A handful decided to stay, and were naturalized into U.S. citizens. Present day Sitka shows pride in its evident Russian heritage.

Ivan Petroff, Counting heads and making enemies

By the winter of 1874, the U.S. Census Bureau determined that the upcoming tenth United States Census should include the region of Alaska, so little being known about it. Through contacts with a San Francisco based historian, Hubert H. Bancroft, the Census contacted a rather slippery character by the name of Ivan Petroff. Petroff was not yet the subject of harsh criticism that would haunt him in later life. In 1874, he worked in Washington D.C., finishing some research for Bancroft. Due to previous Alaskan experience and a command of Russian and English, the Census found Petroff perfectly suited to carry out the Alaskan portion of the tenth annual U.S. Census.

Ivan Petroff had worked with the RAK in Alaska for nearly ten years, later moving to California and slipping in and out of the army, later working for Bancroft. During his time in Alaska, Petroff spent several years stationed at an RAK trading post on Turnagain Arm, not far from Portage Valley.

After delivering his findings and having them printed, Petroff became a magnet for disdain and criticism. He plagiarized William Dall, claimed more travels than he could have actually made, delivered sloppy information about flora and fauna (the census then was far broader than today's headcounts), and presented himself as an authority on native culture, which he was not. However, beneath the chaff, some valuable information emerged, one observation being that the Portage Pass between Chugach Bay (Prince William Sound) and Cook Inlet was still much in use. He added that the glacial activity must have been enormous, so gouged were the mountainsides. It is likely that Petroff had traversed the pass on occasion while stationed on Cook Inlet in the 1860's.

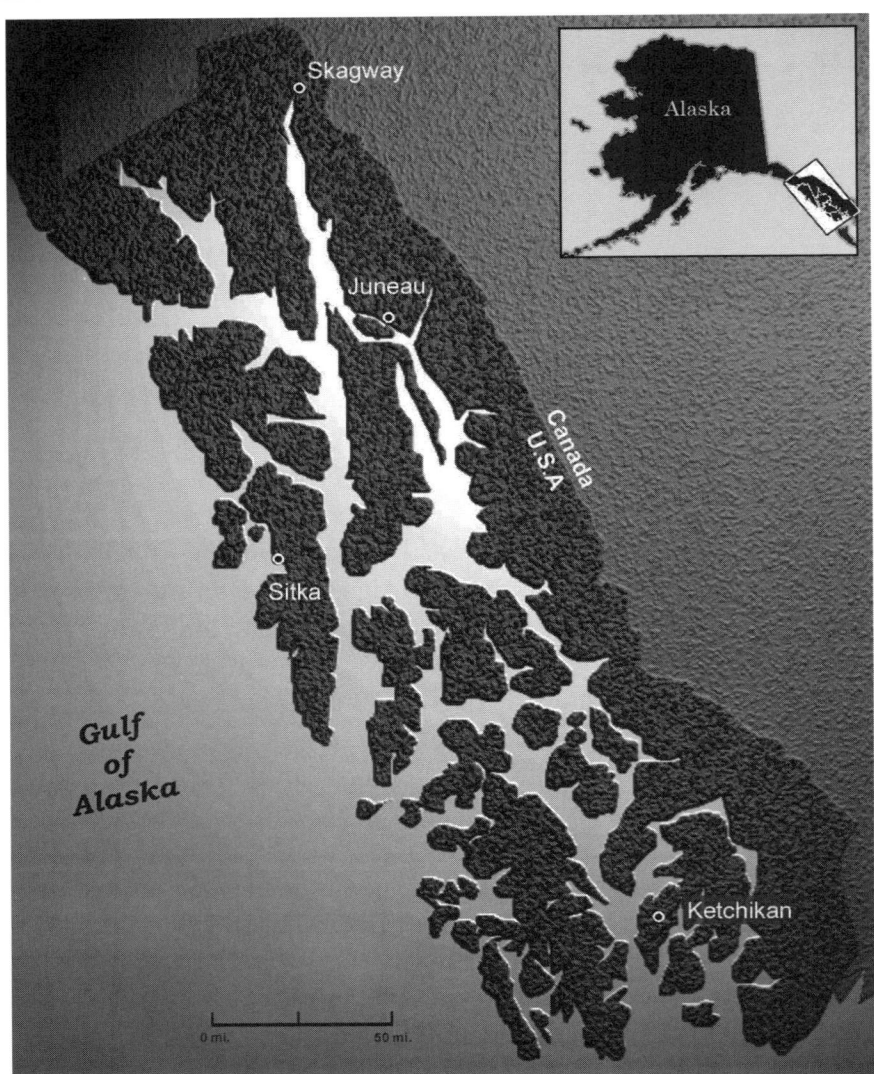

Southeast Alaska, also known as Alaska's Panhandle. In the top center of the map is Juneau, the state capitol. Typical of much of Alaska, even Juneau is rather inaccessible — you cannot drive there, since there's no road access.

While Juneau grew up quickly — as an American town — around it's own private gold rush in the 1870's, Sitka, to the west, had been inhabited by Russian-Americans for over 70 years at that time.

Ketchikan, to the south, began life as a Salmon cannery, and now is an extremely popular tourist destination.

Skagway, to the north, is the gateway town for the Southeast, being only one of two towns in the Southeast with access to roads leading inland. It was also the jumping-off point for gold rushers headed to the Klondike in 1898.

After the Census, Petroff set about to place himself as an eminent Alaskan historian. He published a book titled "Autobiography of a Monk" that has widely been viewed as a forgery. Supposedly a translation of a Russian Orthodox monk's diaries, the "original" was never presented, only Petroff's "translation." Petroff's chapter in Alaskan history closed on that suspicious note.

Hints of Alaska's golden future

With the path across Portage Glacier becoming so well-noted, the area's relative isolation started to vanish. As early as 1848, a team of Russian geologists headed by I.G. Voznesenskii of the Imperial Academy of Sciences found traces of precious gold in the river valleys of the nearby Kenai Peninsula. In 1849 plentiful gold was discovered on the Kenai River on the western peninsula, but the strike was almost immediately overshadowed. Near San Francisco a large gold strike started the stampede of '49 to California. Alaskan gold went unnoticed by the outside world.

William Dall's information and reports on Alaska paired with the promyshlenikis intimate knowledge of minerals available failed to draw many prospectors at first. Only die-hard optimists or those with little left to lose came north before 1867. Alaska was still a wilderness area, as far removed from the contiguous United States as the Moon.

After the 1867 transfer of land, the U.S. Army assumed jurisdiction over what was termed "the Department of Alaska", as it was neither a state, nor a territory, but unincorporated U.S. property. Prospectors and a few homesteaders began to trickle north in stronger numbers, but by 1870, fewer than 1200 Americans could be found in the entire region.

Gold Fever —
Early stage symptoms

Southeast Alaska, being closest geographically, was the first territory explored. Some reports to families back home whispered of promising developments, and Alaska soon had its first gold rush, albeit a small one. A large vein of gold was discovered in a valley near present day Juneau in 1874, and news traveled fast (for the times), drawing the curious and the hopeful north to Alaska. New arrivals discovered a scenario that was replayed year after year in the booming North They discovered that by the time they arrived in gold country, news of the discovery was months or years old, and any good or potential land claims had been staked by others long before their arrival. These dismayed newcomers generally chose one of three paths then, either stay and work for others, go back home, or move on - out to further unproven, unknown, unclaimed lands.

Sunrise — Turnagain's
first community

A few of those who moved on, determined to find their own fortune, wound their way to the Kenai Peninsula. They traveled by sea, sailing around the peninsula up into Cook Inlet. On the north shore of the Kenai Peninsula, bordering Turnagain Arm, small amounts of gold were discovered late in 1874, leading some to settle there. A few who were patient, diligent and lucky eventually made their strike.

The miners on the shores of Turnagain Arm formed a community called Sunrise. News of several large strikes around Alaska drifted into the tiny community over the years, some residents moved on attracted by other possibilities or discouraged by lack of success. Others stayed, and a few struck it big in 1895. The Sunrise strike of 1895 was the first big strike since the Circle City rush of 1893. The final decade of the nineteenth century saw gold fever rising to a high pitch through out

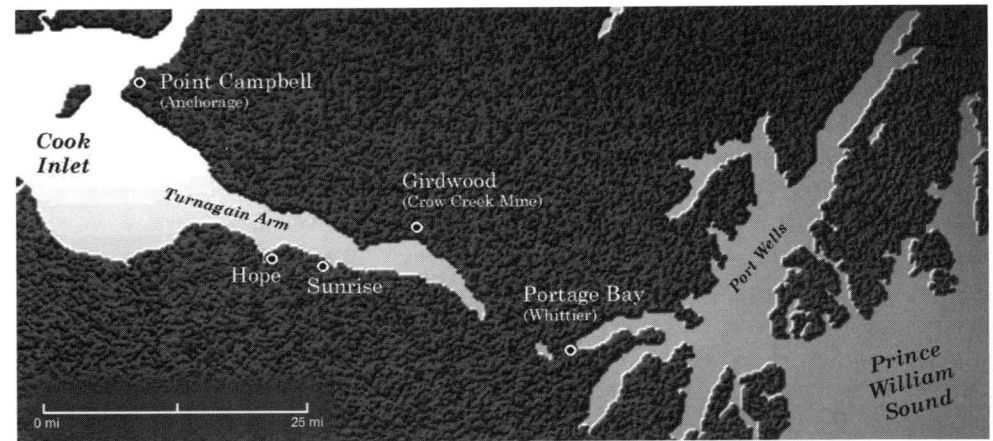

The mining communities of Turnagain Arm. The towns of Hope, Sunrise and Girdwood all sprung up around gold discoveries in the streams of the Chugach and Kenai Mountains.

Much of the travel between these towns and the rest of the world was made by climbing over Portage Pass, and boarding a steamer in what was known then as Portage Bay.

Alaska. Before the turn of the century, the entire world became infected. Sunrise was more accessible than distant Circle City, and the big strike drew larger groups of gold rushers.

Miners and their families from all parts of Alaska made their way to Sunrise before the first snows began to fly. Some mining was possible in the cold months, but the science was still new and chancy, using pressurized steam. In historical perspective, the Sunrise gold rush was small compared to the coming Klondike madness, but South Central Alaska had seen nothing like it at the time. Those settled by late fall set in for a long winter. Winter travel was so difficult as to be impossible, Turnagain Arm was frozen in muddy chunks, and the trails were impassable — choked with as much as forty feet of snow.

The buzz traveling around southern Alaska during the late summer and fall of 1895 spread slowly south over the winter, and word picked up speed. Certain folks already familiar with prior gold rushes were aware that some people always make money during a rush. Regardless of whether any gold is found or not, suppliers make their own fortunes. The support and service providers, merchants and outfitters could always benefit from a captive populace, little competition, and negligible law enforcement.

Frontier government in its infancy

Alaska's district government, a bit over ten years old at this time, generally was held in disdain for playing favorites, legislating under the influence of alcohol and being basically ineffectual. A few of those favorites got together with miners and businessmen from the Sunrise District and met with Governor James Sheakley in a rare scene of cooperation and effort. This gathering sent delegates to Sitka, the regional capitol, to compose a letter to the heads of the Alaska Commercial Company in San Francisco:

The fact that the above request was addressed to the head offices of the Alaska

Sitka Alaska Oct. 30th/1895

Gentlemen,

On Account of the mining excitement in the Turnagain Arm Mining District there will be an increase travel to that country in the spring via Sitka.

The travel has been by sailboat from Puget Sound that being the only way to reach the mines, the Dora not running nearer than Kodiak and Unalaska.

We the Citizens of Sitka and Miners of Turnagain Arm and western Alaska respectfully ask you to:

First - Put a larger boat on to take the place of the Dora
Second - The first trip in the spring land the passengers in Prince William Sound at the portage leading to Turnagain Arm. All other trips run to Turnagain Arm.
Third - to reduce rates.

We would also ask you to assist us to get a Post Office established at Sunrise City, Turnagain Arm.

Commercial Company (ACC), and not to the federal government should give a clear idea of who really controlled daily affairs in the young region.

Though Alaska was young as a U.S. holding, it was and still is an old and immense land. At 365,000,000 acres, it encompasses one fifth the area of the entire lower 48. Less than 60,000 souls populated Alaska as the nineteenth century became the twentieth. These few people spread out over such vast wilderness were governed by four individuals and limited army oversight. A Territorial Governor, a U.S. District Court judge, a U.S. Attorney and one U.S. Marshall plus their meager staff operated out of Sitka, 150 miles from Skagway, 1300 miles from Nome.

Traders, prospectors, miners and natives all had to work out their own disputes, protect their own property, and make life bearable without relying on outside authority. Frontier justice let many small transgressions go unpunished. But if certain serious common rules were broken, such as theft or murder, harsh retribution came swiftly. Rough as it sounds, few crimes were committed, and most of the populace faced more risk of starvation than of being attacked.

The Alaska Commercial Company, a less structured and leaner American version of the Russian America Company took up where the RAK left off. The ACC was still after furs, but its tactics were less violent, more controlled by regulations. Russian cruelty to the Aleuts, Tanaina and Chugach destroyed many lives, families, villages and tribes. As the century changed, the ACC changed as well, trying to become less of a resource-based operation, and more a commercial transport company — servicing the growing population.

"The Bulldog" sails north

In late April of 1896, the long winter began to loose its hold on the Kenai Peninsula. Further south, in Juneau, the SS Dora loaded up with passengers bound for Sunrise City. The Dora, a short tough steamer, was later known as "The Bulldog of Alaska" for its tenacity in treacherous Alaskan seas. She sailed under steam power, yet still bore a pair of working outfitted masts, as a necessary backup.

The normal run of the Dora would take her from Juneau to Kodiak without stops between. However, the ACC decided to comply with the letter of request sent earlier, and scheduled stops in Prince William Sound, in what we now call Passage Canal. They also put a larger steamer on the regular run later, for trips to Turnagain Arm.

April becoming early May, weather would likely have been chancy. If skies were clear, the trip offered lovely scenery, but no record exists of conditions on the

A photograph from high atop Mt. maynard, looking down on Passage Canal in the year 1914. Steamers arriving here with passengers headed to the goldfields landed on the beach in the center of the photograph. The loose gathering of tents that eventually gre on these shores became known as Sullivan's Camp. The townsite of present-day Whittier is mostly off-camera, behind the foot of the first mountain at center right.

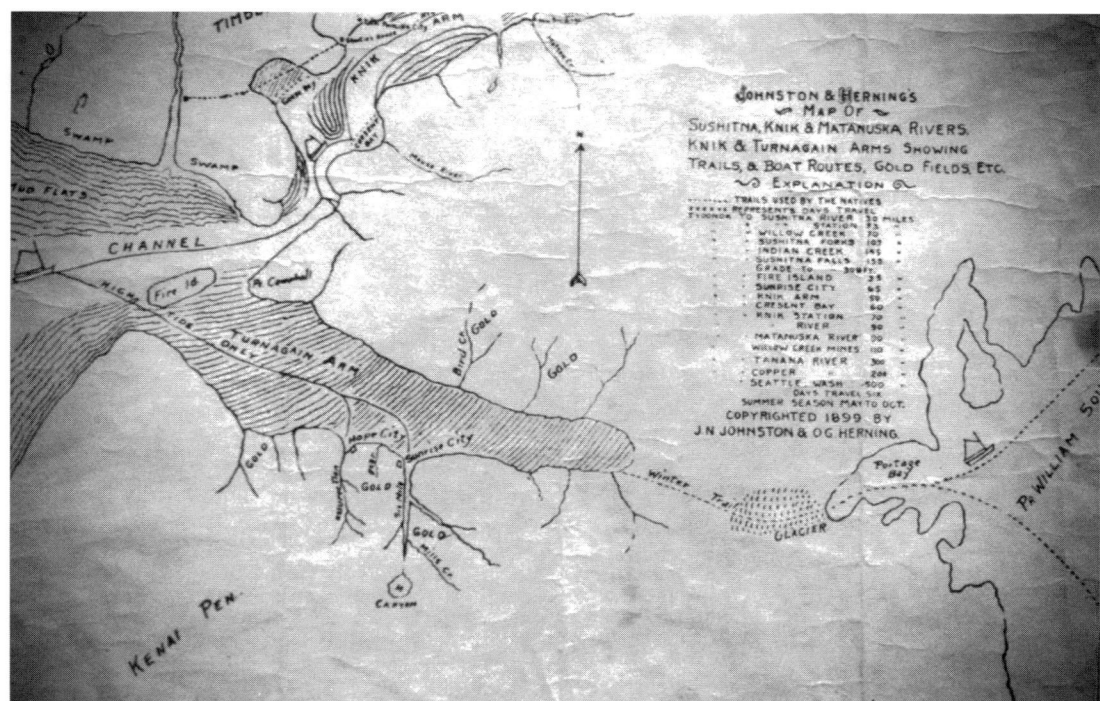

Johnston & Herning's 1899 hand-drawn map of Turnagain Arm's gold communities, and various ways to get there. Though useful to many at the start of a journey, the lack of detailed landmarks made maps like these difficult to use and sometimes dangerous for travelers on foot.

trip. Prince William Sound would still have been relatively full of icebergs, having calved from Columbia and other glaciers. Passage Canal, at the westernmost reach of the Sound, remains ice-free all year. Its counterpart on the east end of Prince William Sound is Valdez Arm, also ice-free year-round. Ice-free harbors proved to be an important factor later in bringing the military to Whittier and the Trans-Alaska pipeline to Valdez.

Sailing close to the head of the Canal, then known as Portage Bay, the mountains closed in, as they had done when the Dora sailed through the straits north of Juneau. Peaks 3,000 to 5,000 feet tall rising out of the green-blue sea. Dark gray stone gave way to dark green spruce, white snow thick on top, patchy snow toward shore and a glimpse of blue-white ice barely visible on glacier faces peeking out under a snow blanket.

If the day had been clear as the Dora landed on the shore of Portage Bay, prospectors would have had a clear view of the portage ahead of them. The base of the trail starts less than a mile from the shore, the crest another mile distant, 750 feet above sea level.

If the day were dreary (more likely), wet snow or rain fell, and little was seen except the dark trees and stones of the shoreline fading away into the gray-white clouds. The group lightered supplies to shore and headed west. One can only guess how they would find their way. Many maps were offered for sale in Juneau, Seattle and San Francisco — but their accuracy ranged from poor to imaginary. A more probable answer to the problem proved to be the assistance of one or two miners or trappers who had made the trip before.

The Dora sailed away from Passage Canal, to Kodiak and Unalaska. She made several more trips to this shore — 400 travelers crossed Portage pass in May alone, nearly a thousand by early fall. The majority of traffic to Sunrise City still came by sea, sailing the long way around the Kenai Peninsula and up Turnagain Arm. By September of 1896 Sunrise City grew to claim a population of 5,000.

The Big Strike happens quietly

The level of economic depression in the United States drove many of these prospectors north, in search of the big strike. Nearby, others dug their own claims hopefully too. That same summer of 1896, 400 miles northeast of Sunrise, George Carmack, Tagish Charley and Skookum Jim hit the big time. They discovered the largest gold strike ever found while on a tributary of the Klondike River. Staking claims in strips across the creek, neighboring prospectors snapped up prime spots within days. Carmack's strike was enormous, but the world waited more than a year to learn of the find, and responded with the great Klondike Gold Rush.

The Sun begins to set in Sunrise

Sunrise had become more than a town, it had become the seat of power for an extended community on Turnagain Arm. Hope, Paystreke and other unnamed camps were all a part of it, extending across the Arm to Crow Creek near present-day Girdwood. None of the strikes in the area

Remnants of a long-ago abandoned cabin, now swallowed up by fireweed, near the town of Hope.

were world-class in size, but a few were big enough to encourage the rest nearby. A few lucky miners managed to claim some paydirt, and set to digging it up, piling it so they could spend the winter months searching through it. They panned the dirt in a heated tent or cabin as the snow blew around them outside. The big snowfalls begin in September, the last regular passenger steamships sailing south in October. After a generally disappointing winter in the Sunrise Gold District, many decided to move on. Some chose to turn back home, some to go further into the wilderness. Many stayed, and of those, a few prepared to head south to resupply for the summer.

Charles Blackstone and the Breakup of '97

Early spring in Alaska goes by the name "breakup." Anyone can tell when breakup begins, as frozen ground breaks into mucky swamps and solid river surfaces melt into chunks and floes. In late March of 1897, well into breakup, a small group departed Sunrise City on foot, bound for Portage Pass and the head of Portage Bay to meet the first steamship of the year. This particular group's crossing became the most famous, or infamous on Portage Pass. The party included four members, J.W. Malingue, Charles Botcher, Charles A. Blackstone and their dog, Sport. The small troupe marched up Portage Valley to the glacier, likely taking the natural trail along the banks of Portage Creek.

As Portage Valley and the Glacier appear today, this journey seems difficult or impossible. However, since the end of the nineteenth century Portage Glacier has been retreating rapidly. In 1897 the Glacier face came right up to where the present visitors center is, very little area being underwater. This land-based valley glacier formed a natural ramp, enabling travelers to climb from the valley floor to the height of Portage Pass (1000 ft). At the Pass, a turn to the southeast pointed one downhill to Portage Bay. By the late 1990's, the glacier has retreated 2.5 miles back up the valley, filling the hollow it created with the waters of Portage Lake.

For foot travelers such as Blackstone and company, the glacial ramp was more convenient than climbing a mountainside, but not by much. The climb proved far from simple, despite the relatively short height and distance. On a fair day the trip might take four to six hours from saltwater to saltwater. On a bad day, one might not survive the trip at all. Malingue, Botcher and Blackstone traveled prepared, all wearing heavy packs, days worth of provisions and heavy warm clothing.

Trails across the glacier were blazed anew every spring, as a winter's worth of snow, landslides and glacial creep eradicated any markers from the previous year. Markers were minimal, usually spruce branches, or small trees wedged into the ice acting as guideposts. The darker the color of the post the better — visibility was often near zero. A light overcast spring day brought an absolute white-out — Bright sun dissipating through white clouds bounces blindingly off snow, ice, glacier

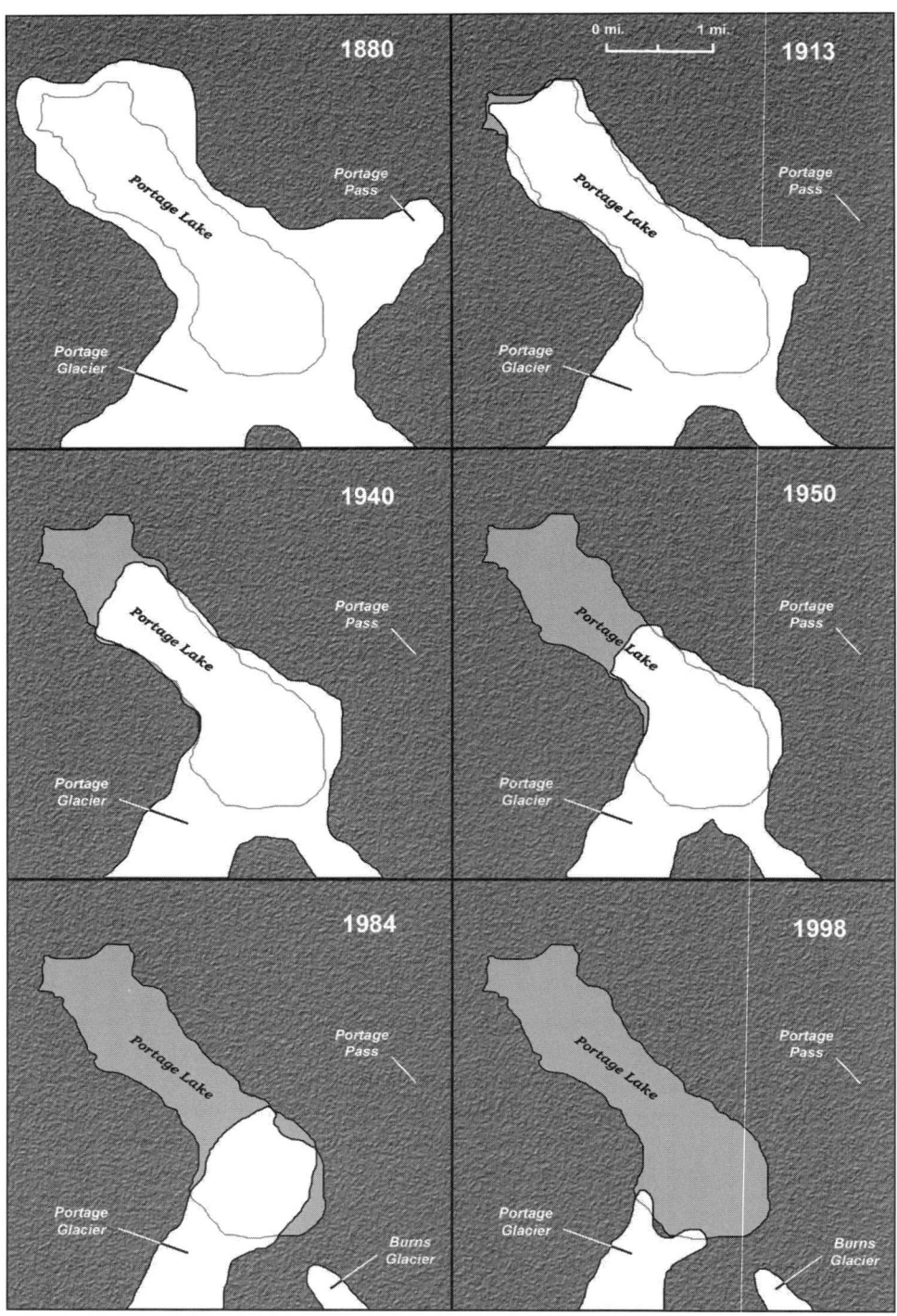

The recession of Portage Glacier. In the past 100 years it has receded nearly 3 miles back into the mountains. Until about 1915, when Portage Lake began to emerge from under the ice, the glacier was useful as a surface for the trail leading to Portage Pass. The length of Portage Glacier is not the only thing that has shrunk over the years — its overall volume, and therefore height and width, has diminished tremendously.

and water while bitter cold winds hurtle along, blinding any unfortunate traveler.

Blackstone's group started their trek in presumably decent weather, as poor weather would have delayed any sane traveler. It was too early in the season for any trailblazers to have placed markers on a good trail, and problems arose quickly. By Tuesday night, March 31st of 1897, Blackstone's group found themselves in desperate trouble. A swift storm had surprised them and already claimed the life of Charles Botcher. The text below is from a note found on the body of Charles Blackstone weeks later, high on a glacial ridge.

party did not disembark, he checked the passenger list. Finding no records of him, Hall set off in search of his friend. Days of sailing brought him to Sunrise City, the last place anyone saw Blackstone alive. It was known that the three men had indeed left for Portage Glacier in late March. Hall's search took him up Portage glacier where, amazingly, he found his friends body, the above note inside his coat. A nearby bay of Prince William Sound, created by a glacier from the same icefield that took his life, now bears Blackstone's name. Blackstone Bay, a popular kayaking destination, lies just south of present-day Passage Canal.

Saturday, April 4th 1897 — This is to certify that Botcher froze to death on Tuesday night. J.W. Malingue died on Wednesday forenoon, being frozen so badly. C.A. Blackstone had his ears, nose and four fingers on his right hand being frozen an inch back.

The storm...overtook us within an hour of the summit and...drove everything we had over the cliff except blankets and moose hide, which we all crawled under. Supposed to have been 40 degrees below zero. On Friday I started for salt water. I don't know how I got there without outfit.

On Saturday afternoon I gathered up everything. Have enough grub for ten days, providing bad weather does not set in. Sport was blown over the cliff. I think I can hear him howl once in awhile.

It is not known whether Blackstone thought he was headed back toward Turnagain Arm or on to Portage Bay, but in reality, he trudged off in a totally different direction, further up Portage Glacier, further from any safety.

In Seattle Charles Blackstone's friend George Hall awaited his arrival by steamer. When Hall saw that Blackstone and his

Fearsome weather and the Turnagain Jet

Instantaneous weather changes are still common in Portage valley, often changes for the worse. Air masses of different pressure, temperature and humidity clash violently right on top of Portage Glacier. One way to picture airflow is to think of it like water flow. High pressure air tends to flow close to the ground, flowing over the ground like spilled water across a tabletop. If the air encounters obstacles, it's more likely to go around them than to go over. If a mass of this air is moving east down Cook Inlet, it is forced into the lowest valleys first.

Portage Valley is not only the lowest pass anywhere between the Kenai and Chugach mountains, but it opens out onto Prince William Sound — an enormous body of water with airmasses of its own. The clashing air masses concentrate over the area around Portage Glacier, resulting in streaming wind tunnels, whirling snowstorms and blinding rainfall. The narrow pass causes a weather phenomenon called a Venturi effect, where high pressure air is forced through a narrow opening and speeds up. Wind speeds up to 150 mph have been recorded through the lower pass. Weathermen and pilots refer to this as the Turnagain Arm Jet (TAJ). Precipitation near Portage Glacier in the warmer months is often accurately described as "horizontal rain", as the wind carries the raindrops sideways quicker than they fall.

Added to the chaotic weather is the fact that the air moving over Portage valley is loaded with moisture, coming from either Prince William Sound or Cook Inlet. The lofty wet air is drawn down toward the glaciers naturally. The air directly above the icefields is cooled and becomes heavier, flowing downhill, creating a perpetual downdraft over glacial icefields. Glaciers become self-generating as cold air draws more snow to their surfaces, building them up, cooling more air and repeating the process.

The Rush is triggered

A few of the residents of Sunrise City who successfully left town headed inland, to a remote unheard-of district in Canada's Yukon Territory, the Klondike. Since most of the good Klondike claims were taken by September the year before, these prospectors became the first in a string of tens of thousands of men and women to arrive in Dawson City only to find disappointment.

Within the Klondike, over 100 miners emerged from their mines and cabins with piles of gold in hand the summer of 1897. They piled onto the first available paddlewheel riverboats near tiny Dawson City in June, and floated down the Yukon River toward the Bering Sea, to St. Michael on the coast. There they boarded the only two steamships bound for the lower 48, the SS Excelsior and the SS Portland. The Excelsior left first, bound for San Francisco. The remaining 68 miners boarded the Portland and sailed in early July for Seattle, Washington.

The Excelsior's landing in San Francisco was not particularly significant, though the passengers were well off financially. A "few more miners" arriving in a town full of jaded prospectors was not novel, and little major news coverage was made of the arrival. However, the evidence of gold became a motivator elsewhere. In Seattle, a newspaper called the Post-Intelligencer received a wire regarding the Excelsior and ran a short story on it quickly. The paper learned of the SS Portland's impending arrival and sent its reporter Beriah Brown to meet the steamer.

Since the Portland had sailed through Canadian seas, it had to clear customs before landing in Seattle. The customs facility was in Port Angeles, Washington, on the north shore of the Olympic Peninsula. Beriah Brown was placed on a chartered tugboat which intercepted the Portland just outside Port Angeles as it left customs clearance. Aboard ship he compiled and wrote the story that set thousands moving north in the months to come. The following excerpt is only the first paragraph:

"ON BOARD THE STEAMSHIP PORTLAND. 3AM — At 3 o'clock this morning the Steamship *Portland* from St. Michael's for Seattle, passed up sound with more than a ton of solid gold on board and 68 passengers. In the captain's cabin are three chests and a large safe filled with the precious nuggets. The metal is worth nearly $700,000 and the most of it was taken out of the ground in less than three months of last winter. In size the nuggets range from the size of a pea to a guinea egg. Of the 68 miners on board, hardly a man has less than $7,000 and one or two have more than $100,000 in Yellow Nuggets..."

Brown's Story went on to tell more about the miners, the land around the Klondike, ways to get there, and cautions against going hastily. He recommended that one ton of food and supplies would be necessary to ensure survival on the trip. His initial estimate of the weight of the gold aboard the Portland proved to be a bit understated. When completely assayed, the total weight came in at more than two tons.

"Grab yer gear and head north!"

The 191 foot SS Portland became the toast of Seattle, and all of her available berths for the return trip to Alaska were filled in minutes. Tens of thousands of men and women sailed north that remaining summer and fall. The year yet to come, 1898, would see the largest migration to Alaska yet. The number of prospectors, businessmen, family members, and onlookers that made the trip is difficult to pin down. Most historical records agree on a number between 15,000 and 30,000 — a number totaling nearly a third of Alaska's population in 1898.

Alaska has remained a favorite destination for world visitors to this day — far more popular with the visitors than with those who choose to stay. Again, a recent set of statistics for historical comparison and reference:

Alaska's total population in 1991: **570,000**
Tourists that visited in 1991: **651,700**

Those who wished to make the journey had daunting obstacles to overcome aside from the geography. Prices for goods skyrocketed in the North. By 1898, a pound of nails cost $8.50 in Dawson City. The Royal Canadian Mounted Police (RCMP) established some rule of law on this frontier, at least as far as admission to Canadian Territory. To cross the border out of Skagway or Dyea, a stampeder had to have not only a hearty constitution, but one ton of food and supplies, as required by RCMP laws. This was an expensive and difficult requirement for most to meet, but was necessary. Thousands of lives were saved by this sage decision on the part of the legendary Mounties.

The well-publicized law requiring the ton of provisions was reason enough to scare off unsure prospectors who had yet to journey north. It also spawned several business ventures, and created a demand that made the fortune of a few businesses that are still around. (Nordstrom's Department Store being one.) Steamship company salesmen roamed Seattle's docks acting as "steerers", making bold sales pitches to the throngs gathered on the streets and wharves. One pitch that sold well was called the "All-American Route" to the gold fields, (despite the fact that the Klondike lay inside Canadian Territory). Five main All-American routes and three "All-Canadian" routes were offered as alternates to the popular Chilkoot Pass or White Pass near Skagway.

None of these routes proved very successful. Trips were often aborted, the stampeders finding that the route existed solely in the mind of the men who sold them the steamer tickets. Some tried to push on anyhow, many dying in the attempt. More were injured, subject to broken bones, exposure, frostbite and snow blindness. Illness played a major role, as typhoid ravaged those in Dawson City, and scurvy struck the majority of miners camped in Valdez.

An early shadow of Whittier

Several steamship companies offered trips to the head of Portage Bay, dropping passengers at the shore armed with little more than an unreliable map, a compass and ambition. The small pocket of shoreline at the base of Portage Pass became a fairly busy campground. Prospectors gathered their supplies for the hike across, dividing piles into manageable loads, stashing what was to be left for later trips. Other folks camped out, waiting for the return of the any steamer to take them south, either to flee the north altogether, or to resupply and return. This little pocket was known as Sullivan's Camp, and was the first semblance of a town in the region later occupied by Whittier. The campgrounds clustered near the site of the present airstrip and tank farm, at the foot of Mt. Maynard.

Advertised "All-American Routes" to the Klondike Gold Fields in Canada's Yukon

   A. Yakutat Bay — route crossing immense Malaspina Glacier
   B. Valdez — sail into Prince William Sound, then cross Valdez Glacier
   C. Portage Bay — crossing the Chugach Mountains to inland trails
   D. Cook Inlet — to the Matanuska Valley, then northeast to the Klondike
   E. Sailing all the way up the Yukon River. (The most costly route by far)

Finding the lay of the land

As explorer W.C. Mendenhall once wrote, there was a "lack of accurate geographic and geologic knowledge of the region lying within the limits of the [Alaska] territory." This evident lack, added to the mass-migration north of American citizens, spurred the U.S. Government into overdue action. Survey teams were dispatched in the spring of 1898, under the jurisdiction of the War Department and the United States Geological Survey (USGS) to make an official reconnaissance and survey of potential and established routes to the interior of Alaska.

Captain Edwin F. Glenn led W.C. Mendenhall and Expedition No. 3 of the Army's group. Expedition No. 2 was led by Captain Abercrombie. Expedition No. 1, a planned trip up the Yukon River, was abandoned due to a shortage of men caused by the Spanish-American War. Abercrombie and his men aimed toward the interior from Valdez, on Prince William Sound. Captain Glenn and Expedition No. 3 were to explore inland from Portage Bay. Sailing from Seattle the evening of April 7, 1898 aboard the SS Valencia, Expeditions No. 2 and 3 arrived in Prince William Sound April 19.

Abercrombie and his No. 3 group split off and landed in Valdez, Alaska — then located on the sandy shore at the head of Valdez Arm. Nearly 700 men filled the encampment. Some rested briefly, waiting to start the trek up Valdez Glacier Others attempted to find alternate outlets to the interior from Valdez. Some assumed a more permanent state of rest, either sick or exhausted from frustrating attempts to get inland. Seven feet of snow on the ground and poor supplies left all parties fairly miserable.

Unwashed men huddled in a few packed cabins and tents, unhealthy and uncertain about their near future. Abercrombie arrived with his team and plentiful supplies. The miners believed relief was at hand and gathered around the military camp. All were turned away, as Abercrombie explained the supplies were only enough for the planned expedition.

An expedition across Portage Pass

An advance party of Captain Glenn's Expedition No. 2 sailed across Prince William Sound to Portage Bay, landing the small steamer Salmo right in the midst of Sullivan's camp, the small settlement that had sprung up there. Dozens of miners met the Salmo, hoping like the men in Valdez that these military men would provide goods and aid for them. They also hoped for settlements of disputes, assistance in packing goods, and for space on the outbound Salmo. The hopeful miners were turned away as they had been in Valdez. Journals of the expedition frequently refer to the disappointed, plaintive prospectors.

The advance party set up a headquarters camp on April 20th of 1898. Four days later, Glenn and the rest of Expedition No. 2 arrived and began explorations the

The head of Passage Canal, known in the 1890's as Portage Bay. This photograph, taken in 1914 shows the tidelands at the shallow shoreline, which later sank several feet during the 1964 earthquake. Mendenhall's group made their base camp on this plot of land in 1898. The piles of gravel to the right are the terminal moraines of Learnard Glacier.

following morning. Under Glenn's command were Lieutenant H.G. Learnard, geologist Walter C. Mendenhall, Lieutenant J.C. Castner and Sgt. William Yanert, among others.

Glenn's group spent four days aboard the Salmo exploring nearby Port Wells, northeast of Portage Bay. Several landings and snowshoe treks confirmed their notion that no practical passes led inland from the bays of Port Wells. The following text concerning those trips is excerpted from the 20th annual Report of the USGS to the Secretary of the Interior 1898-1899:

"The Salmo now returned to the base camp at Portage Bay, and the next day, the 29th of April, I (Mendenhall) joined Corporal Young in a trip across Portage Glacier to the head of the easternmost extension of Cook Inlet, Turnagain Arm. Lieutenant Learnard had already gone across with a small party to investigate conditions about the head of the arm...

"For more than a hundred years it (Portage Pass) has been used as a route, first, by the Russian and Indian traders, and later by miners, who usually cross it without difficulty in the winter or early spring. In the summer the crevasses open and it is but rarely used, especially since at that season the all-water route is so much easier and cheaper.

"On the morning of our first trip across the portage a light rain was falling at the foot of the glacier, but before we reached its highest point we found ourselves enveloped in a blinding blizzard, which obliterated the well-beaten trail and hid completely from our view all landmarks which might serve to guide us. Fortunately the storm was at our backs and helped rather than retarded our progress; but even then, had it not been for bushes which earlier travelers over the same route had stuck in the snow to mark the trail under just such conditions, we should have been hopelessly lost. By noon, however, we were across the glacier and had met Lieutenant Learnard at the foot on the Turnagain Arm side. In the afternoon we moved 3 miles down the valley to the first timber, a clump of cottonwoods, and made a comfortless camp on the snow. Everyone was wet, rain was falling incessantly, wood was scarce and of poor quality, and altogether the outlook was dismal enough.

"The next day, after a vain wait for better weather, it was decided to move 3 miles farther down the valley to Spruce Camp, where more wood, less snow and better shelter were to be found. The move was accomplished with some discomfort, but the new camp itself proved relatively luxurious. It became evident very soon, however, that we were just between the two seasons when mapping or geologic work could be done to advantage. Earlier the snow was firm and fair progress could be made over it with snowshoes. Later it would have disappeared and travel would have been comparatively easy. Just then, however, it varied in depth from a few inches to a few feet, and was so soft and full of water that often a man on his snowshoes would sink to his knees or deeper. Travel under such conditions was so laborious as to be practically impossible.

"Since nothing could be accomplished here, on the 2d of May I returned, in company with privates Blitsch and McGregor, to Portage Bay. We found this trip of 12 miles through soft snow, in which one sometimes sank to his thighs, to be one of the hardest half day's work of the season.

"Later another trip was made across the glacier and back, and although travel along the flats had improved with the disappearance of much of the snow, that on the glacier and its approaches was daily becoming worse with the opening of crevasses, the rise of streams, and the increasing frequency of snow slides.

"During the remainder of May we were confined to the headwaters' camp pretty closely, waiting for the snow to disappear. In the meantime Captain Glenn had satisfied himself that there was no outlet from the northern waters of Prince William Sound toward the interior, and had decided to move the entire command around to Ladd's Station, just above Tyonek in Cook Inlet, and from there investigate the possibilities of a route to the Tanana.

"On the 29th of May Messrs. Kelly and Lampe, with a small party, were started north from Portage Bay to find, if possible, a route to Knik Arm which should be practicable as a mail route during the winter season when Cook Inlet was closed, and the main expedition embarked on the same day for Tyonek.

Kelly did find a trail, though not a very "practicable" one. The Kelly Trail, as it became known, existed mainly as a mapped route and not as a trail. Few have ever traveled it to this day. Starting at Billings Creek on the north shore of Passage Canal, the trail winds slowly into the mountains, then down to Carmen Lake and the Twentymile River Valley. Though Kelly and party did not traverse it further, one could connect to other passes from the Twentymile River Valley, and eventually reach Knik Arm, but only through great effort. The Kelly Trail still exists as an historical route, but was never one of much importance.

Expedition No. 3 in Valdez finally managed to make their way inland via the Lowe River and its canyon. Lt. Castner of expedition No. 2 reached the interior barely alive after traversing the Matanuska Valley and interior, swampy muskeg north of the Chugach Mountains. With the assistance of a band of natives, he returned, having marked out much of the path of today's Glenn Highway.

1898 marked the booming high point of Sullivan's Camp on the shores of Portage Bay. In the following years, historical evidence shows no continuous occupation. The temporary citizens of the camp filtered off to neighboring towns, or back south — "outside" — to the United States.

"Hurrah for the HAE!"

The coastal areas of Alaska would next be examined at a relatively leisurely pace in 1899 by the Harriman Alaska Expedition (HAE). The makeup of the expedition had an Ivy-League air to it, unlike previous rough and tumble explorers. Some of this East Coast academic background became evident in the collegiate names given to glaciers visited by the HAE.

The HAE manifested itself as an interesting turn-of-the-century spectacle. Railroad magnate and millionaire Edward H. Harriman gathered and financed a tour/trip/scientific expedition to Alaska in early 1899. He brought together some 60 botanists, geographers, geologists, ornithologists, taxidermists, photographers, scientists and artists to accompany him in the journey. In addition to the professionals, Harriman brought along his wife, his five children, several friends and a few friends of friends. Harriman purchased a steamer and paid to have it refitted into a luxurious floating laboratory. Work on the ship, the SS Elder, was completed in a Seattle drydock.

The members of the expedition gathered and met in Seattle in the spring of 1899, no doubt soaking in the local madness as gold fever was hitting full stride in the booming northwest town. After the Klondike gold rush, which brought thousands through Seattle's rail stations and ports, two more large strikes made big news, in Nome, Alaska and Cariboo, British Columbia. Seattle had earlier campaigned and established itself as the Gateway to the gold fields of the North, reaping the benefits of thousands of hopeful souls passing through and outfitting themselves. The HAE group boarded the newly refinished 250 foot SS

College Fjord, with massive Harvard Glacier in the center of the photograph. Also visible, from left to right are Bryn Mawr Glacier, Smith Glacier, Baltimore Glacier, Radcliffe Glacier and Eliot Glacier.

Elder and departed Seattle May 31st, 1899. The expedition made frequent stops and excursions along the way, collecting specimens and information throughout southeast Alaska, Glacier Bay, Prince William Sound, the Aleutians and into the Bering Sea.

This mobile group of historians and artists represented one of the last real examples of Major Science by philanthropic industrialists. Carrying on the ages-old tradition of the wealthy and well-educated members of society acting as historian, scientist and artist, they made substantial contributions to the study of Alaska, but covered little territory not previously seen. Their detailed volumes on the insect, sea and tidewater life of Alaska proved very significant to later scientists. Perhaps their most indelible impact was the naming of places and glaciers in Prince William Sound. They sailed into the northwest corner of the Sound, and while exploring the fjords and narrows they named College Fjord, and bestowed names to the many local glaciers, corresponding to the different colleges they hailed from back home. Today one can take a short boat tour from Whittier and see Harvard, Dartmouth, Yale, Columbia, Amherst, Radcliffe, Smith, Bryn Mawr, Vassar and Wellesley Glaciers, among others.

A Surprising find

Toward the southern end of College

Fjord lies a small inlet called Barry Arm. Prior to 1899 Barry Glacier filled a northern valley, crossed the end of Barry Arm and pressed up against Mt. Doran to the south, forming an ice dam. As the HAE sailed toward Barry Glacier, excited members discovered that it had retreated dramatically, revealing a narrow channel between the glacial face and the side of Mt. Doran. The channel opened out into an inlet beyond the glacier, and the decision was made to sail the Elder into the opening.

Steaming into the open, the Elder rounded a corner, and a glacier never seen before appeared to the members of the HAE. They named it Surprise Glacier, and it retains that name today. E.H. Harriman was immortalized in this inlet by having the fjord and the terminating glacier named after him. The same tours that now visit College Fjord often stop in Harriman Fjord as part of the trip. Barry Glacier has retreated miles back since 1899, and the channel is no longer blocked.

Further south they named other glaciers and landmarks, doling out various literary and academic names. The Coast and Geodetic Survey teams would later continue that regional tradition, hence the glaciers surrounding Whittier are named after poets John Greenleaf Whittier, William Shakespeare, Lord Byron and Robert Burns.

The HAE steered the SS Elder out of Prince William Sound, going as far west as the Pribilof Islands in the Bering Strait. On their return to Seattle, July 30th, Harriman and the others were met with much initial praise and interest by the press and public. Reporters discovered that part of Railroad magnate Harriman's intention in sailing north was to search out the possibility of connecting Alaska to Russia by private railroad, boring a tunnel under the Bering Sea to link the rails. Perhaps he realized that linking Siberia and Alaska, two of the most uninhabited areas of the northern hemisphere, would be incredibly unwise and immeasurably expensive. Harriman abandoned plans for a tunnel and returned to New York to bask briefly in the light of his recent accomplishments.

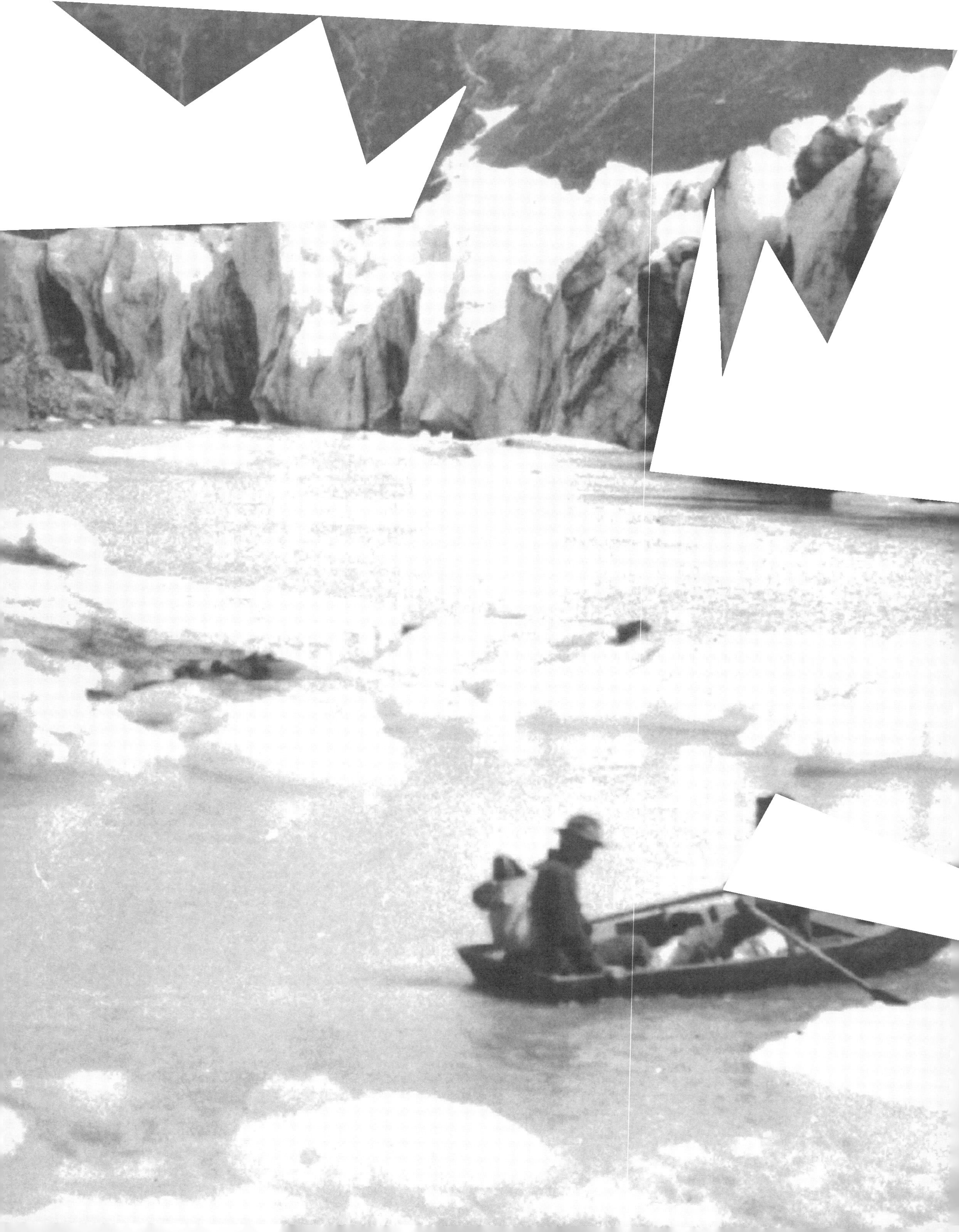

Chapter III
Mapping, Planning & Building — Alaska becomes a Territory

Alaska becomes a Territory, and a home

The HAE's publishings and collections once again focused attention on the distant and still largely unknown U.S. holding of Alaska. The federal government used the momentum of public awareness to make good on election-year promises to further govern the area. In 1900 Alaska was divided into three enormous legal districts. Courts were placed at the seats of power for each district, in Nome, Eagle and the old capitol, Sitka. Frontier justice began to fade, as federal marshals came north.

The following years, the first of the 20th century, saw great numbers of unsuccessful miners heading south empty-handed, more coming north, and a few choosing to make Alaska their permanent home, gold or no gold. 1902 would see the last great gold rush of the era — in Fairbanks — but it was a mere shadow of the Klondike experience. Alaska began to mature from a global curiosity into a home, a productive place. Oil was discovered and the first operating well began production in 1902. The well was near a town called Katalla, located on the eastern Copper River Delta on Prince William Sound.

That same year a telegraph line was completed over parts of the trail Captain Abercrombie had developed, from Valdez all the way north to Eagle, on the Yukon River. Turn-of-the-century Gold production by hand in Alaska hit its high point in 1906, only being surpassed decades later by modern mechanical extraction techniques. Copper, mined for years by natives of the Interior, became the target of industrial miners, and the Kenicott Copper Mine, north of Valdez, opened in early 1911.

Railroad companies look northward

Territorial status was finally granted to Alaska in 1912, and Bob Bartlett became a token, non-voting congressional delegate in the U.S. Congress. Alaska also convened its own Territorial Legislature for representation within its own borders. As part of this congressional attention to the new territory, a commission convened to study transportation problems to and within Alaska. Word spread, and soon railroad companies looked north for possible projects to be commissioned by the government.

The White Pass & Yukon Route RR, a Canadian railway, had been completed out of Skagway in 1900. The fact that it was operational made it unique in the North. "Northern Railroads" abounded, but most of them were only partially complete, or existed solely on paper, or in the minds of a few entrepreneurs — such as the Copper River & Northwestern Route (CR & NW), a partially completed fiasco of a project out of Valdez. An Irishman named Heney

Six members of the Alaska Engineering Commission's (AEC) survey team crossing Portage Glacier in 1914. They carry the tools of professional surveyors, in order to map future planned tunnels to Passage Canal from Turnagain Arm

bored tunnels and cleared paths for a railroad from Valdez to the inland town of Copper Center to be dubbed the CR & NW. The plans fell through for many reasons. The CR & NW came to be known as the "Can't Run & Never Will."

The only other railroad operating at this time, albeit sporadically, was the Alaska Central Railroad (ACRR), which tracked 50 miles north out of Seward. The rails didn't end at a designed terminus, but in the middle of the woods, because the ACRR went broke and the line ceased operation. The Alaska Northern Railway (ANRW) took over and added more rail, extending the line north to Kern Creek, and operated a sporadic seasonal rail service through the Kenai Peninsula. The ANRW was physically and organizationally unstable, but functional. When the federal government commission started looking into inland transportation options they considered building on this line as one possible option.

A first look at a future port

Several business interests sprang up in Southcentral Alaska, responding to the commission's inquiries. A group called the Matanuska & Portage Bay Railroad Company sent engineer F.H. Estabrook on a scouting trip as a locating engineer. As their name implied, this group supported building a rail line from the deep water harbor of Portage Bay through or around the Chugach Mountains to the fertile and coal-bearing Matanuska Valley, some 90 miles distant. Estabrook spent part of 1913 surveying and identifying possible routes out of the old Sullivan's Camp on Portage Bay to Turnagain Arm. His recommendation included one long tunnel, nearly 12,000 feet, through Mt. Maynard, and a cut in the shoulder of the mountain across Bear Valley to the west, (Begich Peak). The Matanuska & Portage Bay Railroad folded without ever marking a trail or laying a single track.

The Alaska Engineering Commission (AEC), a federally organized outfit, sent R.J. Weir into Portage Valley a year later to go over and better survey Estabrook's line. He altered the course of the longer tunnel a bit and recommended a short tunnel through the mountain known as Turnagain Shoulder, (Begich Peak), rather than a cut around the side. Cutting a shelf into the side of the mountain would have left the rail vulnerable to the active face of Portage Glacier. If the glacier surged again it could have easily obliterated any railroad, so

A small boat on a relatively young Portage Lake in 1914. Back then, Portage Glacier had a very active, calving face which still butted right up against Begich Peak (mountain on left). Bear Valley lies behind the glacier, and Mt. Maynard fills the background. Since this photograph was taken, the face of Portage Glacier has retreated more than 2 1/2 miles back up into it's valley, exposing more of Portage Lake every day.

Members of the AEC survey team descend a smooth part of Portage Glacier's surface in 1914. The floor of Portage valley lies ahead of them, with the waters of Turnagain Arm just visible in the distance.

Weir put forward the shorter tunnel idea, which was eventually used.

The AEC sent a large group across Portage Glacier and back several times in 1914, mapping the route in detail. These survey groups were based out of a small camp on ship creek, located 55 miles from Portage Valley, on a low reach of land where Knik and Turnagain Arms meet to form Cook Inlet. This little camp, built on a small muddy creek near a single cabin, grew to become Anchorage, Alaska's largest city. In 1917 Anchorage was named as the main construction camp for the upcoming railroad, and the population grew to 6,500. By 1955 it held 12,000 souls, and by 1990, 230,000 individuals called Anchorage home.

Rails reach the Interior

The AEC made its recommendations at the end of 1914 and in April of 1915 the federal government founded the Alaska Railroad (ARR). President Woodrow Wilson publicly announced the route the ARR would take, and construction began. Portage Bay, though considered for a time as a reasonable terminus, was bypassed. The newly formed ARR patched up the older Alaska Northern Railway tracks out of Seward and connected them to the northern sections, forming a continuous path from Resurrection Bay to the Tanana River in the Interior. Workmen stormed the muddy little Ship Creek valley, looking for work. Many were hired, and the government organized a townsite, out of the mud, for them to live and rest in. Nearly named

Ship Creek or Knik Anchorage, the town became known just as Anchorage. With so much available labor, the main body of construction near Cook Inlet reached completion by late 1917.

The U.S. became involved in the European theater of World War I, and non-essential programs at home were slowed or shelved for the duration, including the ARR. Some work was completed, though very slowly. Working over the winter proved nearly impossible regardless of funding. Finally, in the summer of 1923, visiting President Warren G. Harding rode the line to Nenana, where the rails met, and drove the golden spike, officially completing it on July 15th.

A look at Southcentral Alaska

The demographic mix of Prince William Sound and the Kenai Peninsula was changing significantly. The neighboring Aleuts had been devastated by their interactions with the Russians. Disease, abuse and murder drove a population of nearly 20,000 down to less than 10,000 within 25 years of their first encounters with the promyshlenikis. The Americans could also be abusive, and all traders brought unknown disease, weapons and alcohol with them.

Alcoholism hit the Alaska native population as hard as it had the natives of the rest of North America, with similar tragic results. The native population declined, while the Caucasian population exploded. By 1917 the territory of Alaska claimed a population of 70,000 individuals, one half of which were native, the other half a mix of American, Russian, and British. In the late 20th century though, the native population has been growing at nearly the same rate as the rest of the population.

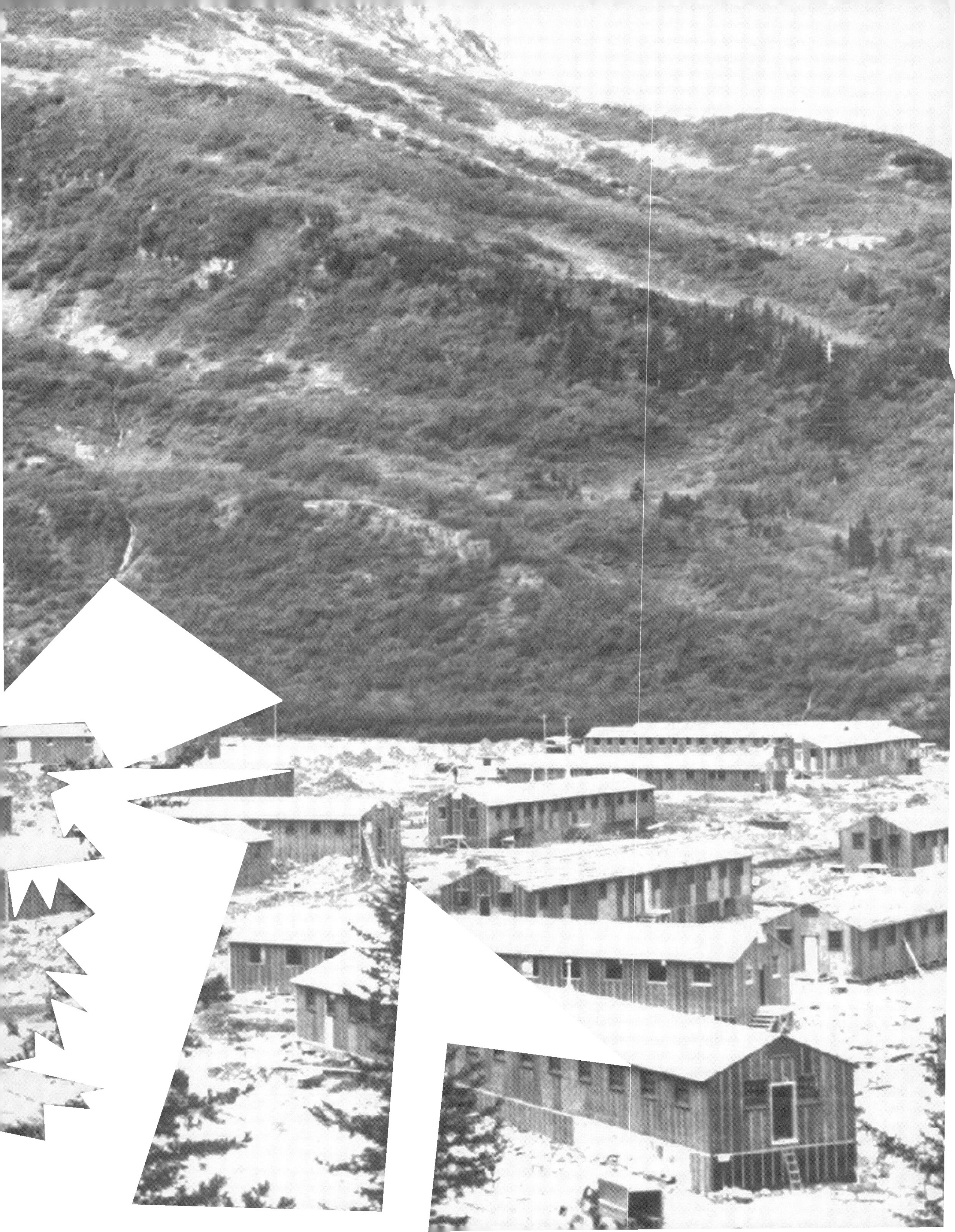

Chapter IV
An Explosion of Development — World War II shapes Alaska

Reevaluations and announcements

By 1940, World War II loomed on the horizon and the U.S. government began to reevaluate the status of all of its outlying territories. Alaska was judged to be both valuable as a defensive point and vulnerable as a target of attack. Plugging the holes in Alaska's vulnerability became a high priority. The isolation of far-flung communities, and of the Territory itself resulted in many logistical problems. The existing railroad section from Seward to Anchorage was labeled a "security risk" due to wooden trestles, bridges and remote locations — easy targets for sabotage. A secure railroad would become a lifeline for any Alaska military operation, and connecting roadways would become a necessity. The U.S. Armed Forces drew up plans and on October 15, 1940 General Simon Buckner announced a series of projects the Army planned to undertake.

"...(A hub) of roads will grow out of Anchorage because of its strategic location as the head of defenses in the Territory. The switching of the railroad from Seward to Portage Bay will also come within the near future, and for the same reason."

The move of the rail terminus would eliminate the risky 60-mile section of track from Seward to Turnagain Arm, shorten transportation time and maintain an easy grade very near sea level. Buckner's announcement received immediate cries of protest from citizens and businessmen in Seward.

The envisioned road system, built nearly as planned, connected Seward to Anchorage, Anchorage to the Richardson Highway (Valdez and Fairbanks) and Anchorage to Portage Valley. At this same moment, planners were examining routes for the Alaska-Canada Highway project, or the Alcan. The planned Alcan would connect Dawson Creek in Edmonton, Alberta to Delta Junction on the Richardson Highway, linking Alaska's roads to the rest of North America. Construction did not start until 1942, but the initial roadway was completed in only eight months.

Early construction begins

Within a week of General Buckner's announcement, the ball was rolling to build a terminal on Portage Bay. Porter Berryhill of the ARR and an engineer by the name of Grammer arranged for tests to be done on the underwater ground structure in the bay. They hired William H. King to tow his pile-driving barge from Anchorage, around the Kenai Peninsula to Portage Bay, and begin to drive test pilings. Berryhill and Grammer pored over the railroad surveys that F. H. Estabrook and R.J. Weir had completed before, and added their remarks, changing little.

Berryhill and Grammer submitted their

surveys to the Army, including plans for the two tunnels. Based on their submission, the rail to Portage Bay and the terminus plans became concrete, despite any of Seward's protestations.

The new rail raises tempers

The spring of 1941 saw initial marking of the rail line and tunnels by hand. The U.S. House Appropriations Committee recommended a bill for $5,300,000 to finance the relocation of the railroad's terminus from Seward to Portage Bay. Citizens from all parts of the Kenai Peninsula were outraged, and representatives from Seward traveled to Washington, D.C. to confront the Committee.

The proposed shift of the ARR terminus from Seward to Portage Bay would make the trip to Anchorage one of 80 miles, rather than the 150 mile trip from Seward. The entire line would be easily accessible for maintenance. Approachable by sea or by land, it lay on an easy grade, either along the shores of Turnagain Arm or on the flats of broad Portage Valley. The existing track through the Kenai Mountains had a number of twisting wooden bridges and tunnels in remote passes. Defense advisors feared that a single bomb or fire could destroy any number of these bridges,

Portage Junction, including the Portage Section House. This is where the existing Alaska Railroad from Seward to Fairbanks would be joined by the short 12-mile spur to Whittier, once the tunnels and rails were completed.

a potential major catastrophe due to the size of some bridges. Repair crews would be hampered by the remoteness of the railbed. Long-term crippling of transportation could last weeks or months, due to the difficulty of rebuilding.

Opponents of the move quickly countered with the argument that if a single bombed bridge could cripple the line for weeks, surely a bombed tunnel — such as the ones on the proposed Portage line — would cripple for months or more. Also, they argued, in a time of need, Seward was an established seaport with existing facilities and an experienced labor force. The proposed Portage Bay terminus existed only on paper, and was a complete unknown. Many of Seward's jobs and businesses were on the line, and they aired their protests before members of Congress.

However, the U.S. Army is rarely swayed by public opinion when the possibility of a war looms on the horizon. With support of the military in Congress, the House and Senate passed the appropriations bill despite Seward's anger, and the $5,300,000 was officially provided April 3, 1941. The money funded the construction of the rail tunnels, 14 miles of track and establishment of a port facility.

Whittier emerges

In March, 1941 the Department of the Interior sent engineers to Passage Canal to plat and survey the new townsite. Names for the future town were tossed around as the surveying progressed. A small community on Turnagain Arm already used the

"Facing Off" the mountain. Workers cut the beginnings of the tunnel into the base of Mt. Maynard. This initial work took place on the Whittier side of the mountain in 1941. Look closely, there are seven men in this photo.

An Explosion of Development — World War II shapes Alaska

name Portage, so another name would have to do. Top contenders were Sullivan's Camp (or just Sullivan) — after the abandoned campsite, Portage Bay — after the formerly named inlet, and Whittier — after the glacier that hangs over the pocket of flat land the town would occupy.

Later, in April, the Army's 177th Engineering group sent 137 military men and 14 civilian railroad subcontractors to meet with the surveyors, and to begin work. The 151 men hiked over Portage Pass from Turnagain Arm, and began working immediately. Primary work was rough, blazing an initial trail through brush and trees. Afterward, official plotted pilot trails had to be cut over the primitive trails.

The first major civilian subcontractor hired by the Army to help construct the tunnels arrived shortly, on June 13th. The West Construction Company of Boston Massachusetts won the contract, partly based on their past record. West Construction had only recently completed and opened the large subway system of downtown Boston, which grew into the massive transport system known today as the "T".

As anyone who has ever worked on any construction project in Alaska can tell you, the season for building is a short one. The earlier a start one gets in the spring, the quicker and easier the job will be finished, hopefully before the first snow of winter. This being said, notice that the U.S. Army and West Construction Co. did not even

The steamer "Aleutian" arriving at Whittier's temporary dock in November of 1941. The temporary dock and most early facilities were at the head of Passage Canal, not far from the tunnel opening.

begin to work on the tunnels until late August of 1941. Using tractors, they began "facing-off" the surface stone for the first tunnel, through the base of Mt. Maynard. Initial boring began on the Passage Canal side, and later work dug from the opposite side.

Poor timing, lack of planning and harsh weather beset all military operations in Alaska and Northern Canada for the next few years. It appeared as if the Armed Forces did not recognize winter as being different from summer in Alaska, and did not make much or any concessions to it.

The rail crewmen that camped on site were primarily tunnelers, but since they were the only ones present, they took on other tasks as the need arose. The campsite was not much to see or to live in, a group of tents and a couple of shacks on the shoreline flat where the airstrip is today. With harsh weather coming, the men needed more permanent shelter. The dock was only a temporary one, and not too practical. Unloading of construction material was described as difficult at best, impossible at worst. These tunnelers soon learned how to be longshoremen, carpenters, architects, electricians, and seamen, as they responded to any problems or incoming shipments or problems that arose.

Tired workmen huddle in the dark inside a tunnel opening. The portal is now awaiting a snowshed, a structure extending out from the mountain to keep any snow or avalanches that come down the mountainside from blocking off the tunnel.

An Explosion of Development — World War II shapes Alaska

"Ever heard of this place?"

The following Army press release was sent out on September 4, 1941:

"EVER HEARD OF THIS PLACE? WELL, YOU WILL
WA D.C. Sept 4 (AP) — The name of "Whittier" was approved by Secretary Ickes today for the townsite to be constructed at the new southern terminus of the Alaska Railroad, originally known as Portage Bay. The name Whittier was suggested by the town's proximity to Whittier Glacier, named after the poet by the Coast and Geodetic Survey."

This short story ran in the Anchorage Daily Times next to a large item about "new all-purpose gas masks" being made available to Hawaiian residents amidst "Japanese Threats." The tension built fast as the danger of war approached. The U.S. remained officially neutral, but for only a few months more.

The residents of the newly dubbed town of Whittier kept busy building the town from scratch well into the deep snows of

A bulldozer clears away stone for access to a new permanent dock facility, closer to the current location of Whittier, in June of 1942.

November. The first major structure completed for the tunnel was a snowshed for its entrance. The snowshed, though small, proved to be a very important structure due to the geography of the area. Where the tunnel enters the side of Mt. Maynard the mountain face is broad, smooth and steep, coming to an abrupt halt at the valley floor, which is practically flat. This forms a very sharp angle, (around 70 degrees). Most snowfall on the slopes of Mt. Maynard slides down, slowly or catastrophically, piling deeply at the foot of the mountain. In order to maintain any access to the tunnel, the snowshed was imperative, and was finished in late November. Tunnelers had already started, and had reached a few yards into the mountain.

A bay by any other name

The body of water that present-day Whittier perches beside was known in 1941 as "Portage Bay." It later became referred to in official papers as "Passage Bay" and the military eventually adopted that new name. Within a few years, however, the common name changed again to "Passage Canal", a name later cemented by usage on USGS and nautical charts. It has, at various times in the past, been called "Chugatskoii Bay", "Chugach Bay", "West Chugach Bay", "Portage Bay", "Portage Fjord", "Portage Canal" and "Passage Bay." Finally, today the body of water remains known as "Passage Canal."

U.S. enters the War

While work continued in Alaska, The United States' other major pacific territory, Hawaii, suffered a hard blow in the December 7th surprise attack on Pearl Harbor by the Japanese Navy. The U.S. declared war on Japan soon afterwards. Alaska lay dangerously close and appeared vulnerable to Japanese aggression. Work in Whittier was pressed, the men learning of the bombing raid within a few days. By January of 1942 the first tunnel stretched 170 feet into the mountain. A second crew was under way on the opposite side, clearing snow and facing off.

As summer approached, the men worked easier, several thousand feet into the mountain. The work was difficult, but methodical, the teams coming together like two slow moles. The rough stone left by dynamite blasts and excavation had to be removed by truck. Finer fill material was trucked back in and laid as a base for the rail bed. After reaching only a few hundred feet in, both tunnels had been ready for track laying, but no track arrived on site until well after the first tunnel was completed. The laid rail would have made movement much easier and completion quicker, but the war situation delayed and diverted many supplies meant for the tiny military camp in the woods.

Occasionally the delivery of materials wasn't too late, but far too early. Such was the case when a steamship landed with more than one million board feet of lumber to be used to build a permanent dock. When the lumber ship arrived, it docked unannounced, a complete surprise to the entire post. Temporary storage for the lumber had to be constructed. No power or other tools were available to process the lumber. The offloading of the ship via the rickety temporary dock took more than five days, with all crews working 'round the clock.

Japan attacks Alaska

The world's eyes focused briefly on Alaska in June of 1942, as the Japanese Navy staged an attack on American soil for the second time. Carrier-based bombers flying from North Pacific locations carried out two missions to bomb the town and base of Dutch Harbor on Unalaska Island in the Aleutians. Though many bombs hit close to their mark, the relatively new Navy base on tiny Amaknak Island in Unalaska Bay was not permanently damaged. The wide scattering of bombs did cause heavy casualties, 75 civilians and soldiers were killed.

In a tactic used throughout WWII in the

The upper end of the Whittier Garrison, September, 1943. Dozens of wooden bunkhouses and support shacks line the streets of the newly built military town. Nearly all evidence of these buildings existing is now gone — as they were either torn down or replaced with concrete structures.

The new "permanent" dock facility under construction. Built in deeper waters than were available at the head of Passage Canal, this dock would allow much larger ships to tie up directly alongside a pier that was close to land. The smoke in the photograph rises from a floating piledriver.

Pacific, the Japanese military forcefully occupied small outlying islands, establishing a base for further attacks. Though it was not known at the time, the whole Japanese attack on Alaska was a diversion. The bulk of the Navy was massing in the South Pacific for a planned masterstroke. The failed campaign had hoped to destroy the entire U.S. Pacific fleet in one single massive attack.

Unalaska Island was heavily fortified, and lay close to Anchorage. The Japanese chose to occupy islands further out, tiny Aleutian Isles called Attu and Kiska. Only Attu harbored a measurable population, which was unable to defend itself. The Japanese deported the inhabitants to prisoner camps along with thousands of other prisoners, far to the south. In a short time the occupation force swelled to 14,000 Japanese soldiers on the two islands, with control over several unoccupied neighboring isles.

American response was to reinforce the military in Anchorage and Dutch Harbor, to put pressure on the Japanese with a block-

Rail work camp, (above) on the Whittier side of the longer tunnel. The waters of Passage Canal can be seen in the upper left.

Small rail cars in the center of the photo carry fill material out of the tunnel during drilling operations. You can see the newly dumped fill at the end of the rail in the upper right of the photo (the dirt with no snow on it).

The odd structure at the bottom center is the top of the snowshed, at the entrance to the tunnel.

Fill dirt and grading for the railroad tracks (left) which will be arriving soon. The structure in the center is the end of a temporary rail that leads back to the tunnel entrance — used to bring the material out of the tunnel.

A steel hulk of a long-deserted ship lies grounded at the head of Passage Canal.

The view from the top. Looking down on Passage Canal and the west tank farm from the high point on Portage Pass

Rails made into twisted ribbons by the 1964 earthquake. This photo was taken near the town of Portage, and is part of the rail that connects Whitier to the rest of Alaska.

College Fjord, (above), filled with small icebergs, with Harvard Glacier (largest), Bryn Mawr Glacier and Smith Glacier

The devastated waterfront of Whittier, (above), just days after the 1964 earthquake. The rusted masses in the foreground are what's left of the old tank farm, lying amongst the blackened debris left behind after the Tsunamis and fuel oil fire.

Interior of the Buckner Building, 1994. Pictured (left) is one of the rec rooms for enlisted men. The Buckner had been left idle and exposed to the elements so long that mossy grass had taken root in the standing water on the floor of this 3rd-floor room.

Fog shrouds the surface of Turnagain Arm, as seen from the top of Mt. Alyeska on a subzero February morning. The mountains of the Kenai Peninsula lie across the inlet, the Girdwood Valley occupies the foreground

Remnants of the theater facilities inside the Buckner Building. The two-story tall theater was outfitted to both show movies and to host theatrical performances.

Bear Valley in Autumn, before the construction of the new road. Placer Creek, in the lower right, empties into Portage Lake, center. Pilings from an old rail trestle lie on the creek shore. Byron Glacier is just visible in the distance, emerging from the low clouds.

A pile of tidal wreckage on the shores of Passage Canal. Pilings, planking, driftwood and bent rails lie tangled together in a natural archaeological history of Whittier — one part railroad, one part buildings and docks, four parts Mother Nature.

The Alaska Railroad's Portage Shuttle, ready to make the 12-mile trip to Whittier on a sunny winter morning. 4,000 foot tall Blueberry Hill catches the light of the sunrise in the background.

Whittier's small boat harbor, dock and the Buckner Building, viewed from Learnard Creek.

Military crews in Portage valley lay down rail ties and tracks in the snow in January of 1943.

ade of Attu and Kiska, and to speed work on the Alcan and the Whittier tunnels. By August of 1942, Navy forces and massive bombing moved the American front line to nearby Adak Island. From Adak, bombing raids were launched against the occupiers, and a long winter campaign began.

The bitter winter conditions arrived, 1942-43 proved to be a particularly harsh season. The Japanese soldiers hunkered down on their small possessions, thousands of miles from home or relief. The U.S. Navy maintained the blockade and the bombing raids throughout the duration. The weakened Japanese Navy did not attempt any major run of the blockade, and both sides waited for the daunting weather to die down.

Whittier is electrified

Construction continued apace in Whittier. Earlier in the summer, a military bomber flying out of Anchorage made a low pass over Portage Valley to Passage Canal. As it passed, the bomber dropped a load, not of bombs, but of electricity. A spool of heavy electrical wiring had been rigged in its bomb bay, a weight tied to one end. Crewmen dropped the weighted end as the bomber flew slowly over the construction camp in Portage Valley, and the wire fed off the spool as the weight hit the ground.

The wire played out, laying over the top of 3,500 foot Mt. Maynard, the end finally dropping into the camp-town of Whittier. The Portage end of the wire was connected to existing power lines, providing a link to the distant construction camp. Working circuits became possible through the

The arrival of the first passenger vessel to Whittier's new permanent dock facility in June of 1943. This same docking facility is still in use today.

following winter, when the lines broke somewhere on the snowy mountaintop.

The troops currently in Whittier acted only as a construction crew. October 3, 1942 marked the first official stationing of U.S. troops in Whittier. Lieutenant Robert Peters and 15 enlisted men of Company C, 297th Infantry, Valdez became Whitter's first troops, arriving by sea from Valdez. They lived in tents in the construction camp, as barracks had not yet been constructed. Guards were posted immediately, as Whittier was classed a military installation during wartime. A month later Company C's 42nd Engineer Group arrived, and its Captain E.K. Staley assumed command of the new Whittier Garrison. This large group also occupied the tent campsite on the rocky shores of Passage Canal.

38 year old Captain B.B. Tally arrived on the scene shortly after, having just successfully completed construction of an air base in faraway Yakutat. Tally, as head of the Alaskan engineering division, became directly involved in the tunneling efforts, and would later design and build Anchorage's Elmendorf Air Force Base.

Work on Whittier's permanent dock was

well under way by November, 1942, but having started late in the summer, the work slowed as the first winter snows fell. Military planning once again timed the start of a big project poorly, finishing in bitter cold. Supplies still arrived sporadically, and much needed pilings were unavailable for more than a month.

The only death involved with the construction of the tunnels occurred in late 1942. B.B. Tally labeled it a "freak accident", as a lone workman had been walking through the longer (Passage) tunnel, a single large rock broke loose from the ceiling, crushing him. The man died instantly. The loose rock was an unusual occurrence due to the fact that the entire mountain was essentially one single stone. A mix of graywacke, slate and shale, referred to as the flysch of the Prince William Sound terrane, the stone is similar to large-grained granite in structure and strength. This uniformity of strength made tunneling and supporting the tunnels relatively stable.

Whittier Garrison from above, 1943. The permanent dock facility is visible in the middle distance, as well as the dozens of semi-permanent wood and canvas structures that made up the living quarters, operations, storage and mess facilities. The small structure visible in the center right, just up in the forest, slightly above town is a small hydroelectric facility, generating some of the new garrison's power.

An Explosion of Development — World War II shapes Alaska

Temporary Rail headquarters in Portage Valley during the construction of the second tunnel, through Begich Peak.

Notice the specially-rigged automobile in the bottom center, designed to drive the rails.

Completions

On October 25, 1942 the 1500 mile long Alaska Canadian Highway was completed, linking Alaska to the rest of the world by a long tenuous ribbon of mud that took years to mature into a highway. Some still consider the term "highway" to be wishful thinking.

As November passed the halfway mark in Whittier, excitement grew as the two teams on opposite sides of Mt. Maynard lay within just a few dozen feet of meeting. Would the lines be straight? Would the tunnels meet at all? Would the grade be constant? Workers concurrently building support timbers for the tunnels, the permanent dock, the barracks next to the dock and the road bed for the rail to follow from tunnel to dock, all paused briefly one morning as an announcement was made.

At 11:18 am on November 20, 1942, the Passage tunnel was "holed through." The teams met, and all crews celebrated briefly — as the centerlines of both tunnel crews met cleanly in the middle, missing dead center by less than a foot. The tunnel's official length is 13,086 feet. The shorter tunnel, through Begich Peak, referred to as the Turnagain or Portage tunnel was holed through soon after, coming out at 4,912 feet long.

At over 2.6 miles long, Passage tunnel remains one of the world's longest rail

Major General Simon Buckner, head of operations, is at hand to throw the switch for the final blast in the longest tunnel on November 20, 1942. The first trains would roll through five months later.

tunnels. It runs straight as an arrow from one end to the other. When the crews holed through, the only light they saw came from lanterns or tractor headlights. When standing dead center in the middle of the unlit tunnel, the light at either end appears as a distant dim point of light. One person described it as being "like standing outside at midnight and seeing only two stars, one in front and one behind you."

Construction on Passage tunnel lasted for 309 days, digging an average of 25 feet every day. Nearly 100,000 cubic yards of rock were removed using over 525,000 pounds of dynamite. Work on the rail bed continued, connecting the two tunnels through tiny Bear Valley, and on to Portage Station.

Not only were the tunnels, railbed and barracks nearing completion, but the terminal railyard and dock went into full construction in the winter of 1942-43. The small flat shelf that present-day Whittier sits on was perfect for the space require-

Whittier's first rail passenger station, at the foot of the recently built Whittier Manor, on the right.

ments of a rail switching yard. Many tracks were laid side by side, merging at the west end, allowing trains to be "built" car by car before being pulled to Anchorage or Fairbanks.

Enough steel arrived to begin laying track in the tunnels on December 31, 1942. Progress was smooth, though cold, as no snow filled the tunnels, but a nearly constant wind blew as air rushed from one end to the other.

Work conditions warmed a bit by the spring of 1943, and a series of projects reached completion. The permanent terminal dock officially opened, ready for full use, despite the fact it had been in full use for several months already. Anton Anderson, Chief Locating Engineer for the Alaska Railroad, and head of the Whittier field office for construction, oversaw work on the dock and completion of the switching yard and grade to the tunnels. He was as much of an old hand at Alaska Railroading as was possible. He formerly worked on the original Alaska Railroad project in 1917 for several years, had worked on the Great Northern Railroad further south, and now headed the Whittier segment of operations. The rails nearly in place, Whittier lay on the brink of connecting to the rest of Alaska.

Activation and Inauguration

In Anchorage, the headquarters of the Alaska Defense Command issued General Order No. 39 of 1943, officially activating Whittier as an Army Post. The activation came just before the last rail was laid and secured. The final procedure necessary was a thorough checking of the gauge, (width), over the length of the track.

Anderson's counterpart on the Portage side, a man named Olavi V. Kukkola, took 14 workers with him and rode the inaugural train to Whittier on April 23, 1943. The first train left the existing ARR tracks at Portage station, and traveled 14 miles to the newly christened Whittier Army Post.

Celebrations were necessarily short, as more work needed to be done, expanding Whittier from a mere functioning terminus to a full Army base and dock facility. The span of time from the landing of the first group of railroad workers to the rolling through of the first train was exactly two years — April 23, 1941 to April 23, 1943.

Ending a year of Japanese occupation

In World War II, Alaska stepped into the forefront of the world's attention again in May 1943. U.S. forces in Alaska massed for the retaking of Attu and Kiska, occupied for nearly a year by the Japanese. Continued blockading had taken its toll on the occupying forces, and other than a few small evacuations, Imperial Forces in Tokyo had left the 9,000 remaining men to survive on their own.

Tanker trucks, boats and supplies are carried inland towards Anchorage by an Alaska railroad steam locomotive 501 in June of 1943. (Photo formerly classified).

On May 11, the U.S. landed 17,000 troops on Attu Island, a hilly rocky stronghold. Heavy shelling and ground combat pounded the 3,000 Japanese soldiers in the upper hills. By May 29, the U.S. had suffered 550 deaths, and the Japanese lost over 2,200. The 800 left alive staged one last charge, overrunning American positions and throwing the offensive lines into confusion. Quick opposition by the better supplied, healthier U.S. forces and reserves led to victory, and the U.S. retook Attu.

Out of the 3,000 Japanese men who occupied Attu, a mere 28 survived to be taken prisoner. It foreshadowed the suicidal tenacity that led to so many more deaths on both sides in the South Pacific later in the war.

For the rail workers, May and June in Whittier were easier, though no less busy, times. The first Army troops were permanently assigned to the new base, and most facilities reached completion, including the new barracks, the dock building and a permanent electrical link through the tunnels. Most structures were wooden, some with concrete bases. Troops began arriving as construction crews departed slowly. Command became shared between the Quartermaster's Office of the Army and Anderson and Kukkola — the field office engineers.

Preparing for Kiska

Back in the Aleutian Islands, U.S. and Canadian forces prepared for the more daunting task of retaking Kiska Island. Japanese numbers on Kiska were twice that on Attu. Nerves tensed as re-occupation forces faced the prospect of fighting uphill against over 6,000 fanatic troops. A number of extremely foggy days in July fueled suspicions that the Japanese Navy may have brought in reinforcements, evading blockade ships.

On August 15, 1943 the combined U.S. and Canadian troops landed 34,000 men on the shores of Kiska to fight an unknown number of opposing forces. The Canadians landed on one side of the island, the U.S. on the other. Shots were fired, explosions heard and confusion reigned. Cooler heads called a halt to the shooting, and in the silence it was discovered that the Japanese Navy had indeed slipped through the blockade in the fog, but not to reinforce, only to evacuate. No Japanese troops remained, but evidence of their stay surfaced everywhere. Nearly every item of interest left behind was booby-trapped, causing numerous injuries and deaths. The Canadian and U.S. soldiers had mistaken each other for the enemy and fired their weapons. In the absence of any opposing troops, 94 men were killed and 80 injured by mistakes and booby traps. Kiska was retaken, and the only armed occupation of U.S. soil in history came to an end.

Whittier — the newest cog in the War Machine

Whittier, already in a position to assist, began to service the repositioning of equipment that followed the end of the

Aleutian campaign. Materials were flown to Anchorage, placed on trains and shipped to the docks in Whittier. Once the material arrived, workers began loading transport ships and barges.

The workers in Whittier started feeling an air of permanence settling in as days wore on, developing a sense of community as the base grew in size and capability. Whittier's first newspaper in was printed in October 1943 — a four-page mimeographed newsletter titled "The Dockwalloper."

Winter arrived late in 1943, but blustered in harshly. Heavy snows set records throughout Prince William Sound. On January 6th of 1944, a visiting USO troupe staged a show for the men of Whittier as they waited to board their transport. The star of this particular show was none other than Ingrid Bergman. At the time Bergman arrived, 8 feet of level snow covered the ground, the temperature hovered near 0 degrees and gale force winds blew in from Prince William Sound. The barracks were unaffected by the weather, and Ingrid's show went on.

ports, Whittier primarily acting as a military facility.

The last few construction sites closed down in the fall of 1944. The Whittier field office, after having fulfilled its main purpose, transferred the few remaining construction tasks to the Army post engineer who remained permanently stationed in Whittier.

The German Army surrendered to the Allies in Berlin on May 8, 1945. Later that year, in September, twin nuclear bombings forced the Japanese to submit to the Allied Forces as well, ending World War II. The war brought more development and modernization to Alaska than any previous event or effort. New military facilities had sprung up in Dutch Harbor, Anchorage, Whittier, Fairbanks, Kodiak, Attu, Sitka and parts of the Kenai Peninsula. New roads connected Anchorage to Seward, Fairbanks, Valdez and the rest of the U.S. and Canada. Young men by the thousands were introduced to the Great Land courtesy of the U.S. Army, many choosing to stay, or to return after their tour of duty was completed.

Conclusions

The remainder of the war years saw Whittier mature as a port, but did not see a massive expansion. Despite earlier fears and cries from Seward, Whittier did not gain a monopoly on rail service out of Anchorage. The increased traffic due to the war was divided evenly between the two

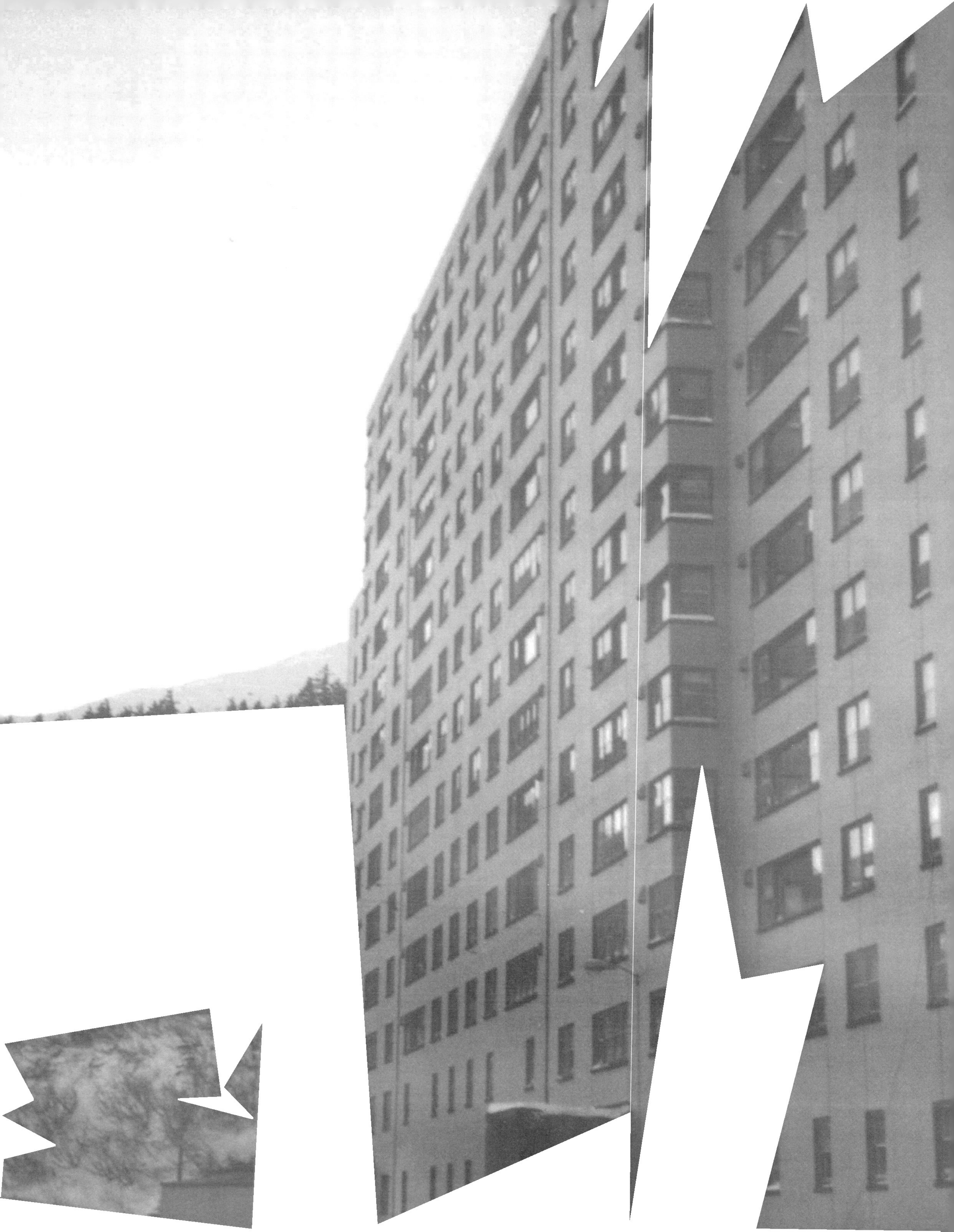

Chapter V
From Massive Plans to Meager Ends

Planning a future Whittier — on a Grand Scale

Assessing post-war needs and policies, the military decided that the port of Whittier was an excellent success, and committed to developing it into a large functional permanent base. A complex of ten concrete buildings was drawn up. The massive reinforced structures would be connected by underground tunnels to avoid the extreme weather. The post-war atmosphere of uneasiness with the U.S.S.R. gave Alaska a further boost as a U.S. defensive priority. At their closest point, Alaska and Russia lie less than 15 miles apart. The plans for Whittier were assigned to architectural divisions and made ready. The wooden structures that made up the present Army Post soon became construction barracks once more.

Supply ships and work crews began arriving in the spring of 1949. The final platting complete, construction was slated to begin. The complex at Whittier would consist of three massive buildings and seven smaller support structures. Most of these would be linked by heated underground passages, drilled through the same sort of stone that had made up the railroad tunnels. Connected underground, there would be little need to keep snow clear for movement from building to building.

The buildings were planned as:

A. A composite housing / service / recreation facility
B. A multipurpose receiving / shipping / storage facility to be added to a new heavy capacity shoreside dock
C. A large family housing unit apartment complex
D. Several smaller support facilities, including a post headquarters, a communications building and a central heating/power plant.

"A city under one roof"

Initial construction beginning in 1949 concentrated on the power plant and the housing / service / recreation center. The latter, an enormous building, soon materialized as the largest structure in the entire Territory of Alaska. It was called the Buckner Building, after General Simon Buckner, however construction documents refer to the monstrosity as "It", "the building", later "Buckner City", "The Buckner" and "Bucky." The Buckner was often referred to as a "city under one roof." For convenience in the harsh weather and small area of buildable land, (97 acres of flat ground), one massive consolidated building was conceived, with services that would fill every need a small community might have. The Army built it at a cost of $6,000,000.

The Buckner rises six stories above ground, with two below — 273,660 square feet at 525 feet long and 160 feet wide. A

The Buckner building, as it appeared in 1997. The Buckner has 273,660 square feet under one roof, and was called "A City under One Roof". Among its amenities were a rifle range, bowling alley, movie theater, and a radio station.

lengthy list of most of its facilities includes: comfortable housing for over 1,000, a 540-seat cafeteria, classrooms, a rifle range, a 350-seat theater (for both live performances and movies), a radio station, a photographer's darkroom, a four-lane bowling alley, a library, a hobbyshop, a post office, a post exchange, a barber shop, a snack bar, a massive kitchen, a bake shop, a church, a six-cell jail, a guard house, enlisted men's day rooms, noncommissioned officers lounges and a large infirmary, made up of an operating room, x-ray clinic, pharmacy, seven examination rooms — private and semiprivate and a 4-bed ward.

Moving around indoors was made easier by central hallways on each floor running the length of the building. It has eight different stairwells, four passenger elevators and 2 service elevators. The outer ends have seven separate fire escapes.

Decoration was sparse, as the entire design was more utilitarian than artistic. This resulted in a typical, though large, structure of the Cold War U.S. military — concrete gray, 1950's style pastel interiors, clearly labeled doors and offices and a uniformity of style throughout. About the most festive decor to be found throughout was a wallpaper pattern in a music-listening room off one of the day rooms. The pattern of two 1950's teeny-boppers, in a repeating white outline, danced by a record player against a black background.

The architectural aspects of The Buckner are unique as well. The whole structure is made up of seven different sections. Each section is separated by an eight-inch gap on every floor. The separate sections allow the Buckner more give — an easier ability to move with an earthquake — rather than have it fail, as a solid monolith might, in a bad shake.

The roof is flat, occupying 35,000 square feet. In order to deal with the thick snowfall, a modern (1950's) snowmelt system was built into the roofing, with central drains to catch all the meltwater and keep the roof clear. Even so, in winters with heavier snowfall shovelers still had to go topside to prevent any buildup that might cause a collapse.

Ground-breaking for the Buckner building was held in 1950, the majority of the work being finished in 1952. It was officially opened by the Army in early 1954.

Southcentral Alaska grows into the 1950's

As WW II had sped along Alaskan Development, creating an urgency to

Left open to the elements since shortly after its abandonment by the military, the Buckner building has suffered much superficial damage at the hands of Whittier's rough weather over the past 30 years.

complete tasks, so the Korean Conflict added speed and value to Whittier's new buildup. The summer of 1950 saw the first heavy involvement of U.S. troops as a part of U.N. forces in South Korea. The war in Korea became a focus of Cold War instability, of western U.N. forces fighting Soviet/Chinese communists. Alaska's closeness to the U.S.S.R. became even more significant as the Arms Race built and parts of the Distant Early Warning (DEW) missile defense systems were constructed within the state. The drive to bring Alaska up to speed as a defensible territory and an modern front-line observation center brought military men and equipment back north through again, using Whittier's port as a main point of entry.

Seward jumped ahead of Whittier once again in competitive positioning as the last mile of the Anchorage-to-Seward Highway was paved in 1951, opening up the Kenai Peninsula. The Alaska Department of Public Roads drew up proposals to extend the highway to Whittier, but the costs exceeded the present needs.

The influx of military and civilian construction personnel into Whittier proved to be more than the quickly aging wooden barracks or the unfinished Buckner could hold, so under the direction of the Federal Housing Authority an 80-unit apartment house was constructed on a hillside just east of the Buckner site. The building is still in use, called the Whittier Manor, and now houses a small chunk of the permanent population. Rental rates for apartments in 1950 were posted as $95-$150 per month.

The outer sections of the Buckner building were completed in the summer of 1952, and the job of interior finishing began. The dock facility also reached completion at this time. It was made up of a 900 foot-long concrete-surface deepwater dock with an adjacent 87,000 square foot, two-story receiving/shipping/storage building. Ground breaking also began for the family housing unit, to be called the Hodge Building.

Whittier's "other" monolithic structure

The "Hodge", (now known as the Begich Tower or — or the BTI), was completed in early 1956. It rose 14 stories above the shore and was the tallest building in Alaska. It is still tied with the top three in the state, since statewide construction guidelines keep building heights low due to the threat of earthquakes. The Hodge, when finished, was 14 stories, 265 feet long by 110 feet wide and had 177 apartment units, with either 1, 2, or 3 bedrooms for military families. 39 bachelor apartments were built in, as was a playroom, two lounges and a snack bar. Each of the apartments were self-contained, with a kitchen, bath, living room and a dining area. For earthquake reasons, it was also built in sections, as the Buckner had been, with eight-inch gaps in between. Twin underground tunnels connected the Hodge to the Buckner, one for service, heating, cables and plumbing, the other for foot traffic.

Originally called the Hodge Building, and now known as the Begich Tower, this 14-story structure (left) was at one time the tallest building in Alaska.

Built for family housing, it was the final piece in the overall plan to make Whittier a permanent and hospitable Military base — completed in 1956, only four years before Whittier was inactivated.

A photo (below) of the Hodge Building just days after the 1964 earthquake — showing no outward damage at all.

Whittier reaches its high point

The hostilities in South Korea ceased in the summer of 1953, and the U.S. pulled its forces out to return home. The full 10-building Whittier complex had been scaled back during construction, to eight buildings total, avoiding redundant facilities. The mid-50's in Whittier became a time of completions, with the completion and transport of the troops from South Korea, the official opening of the Buckner, completion of the Hodge and refitting of the old dock into a fuel-oil terminal with a nearby shoreside petroleum tank farm. Petroleum tanker ships sailed north from the lower 48 to arrive in Passage Canal and offload oil into waiting tanks. Later the oil was loaded into railroad tanker cars and shipped north to Anchorage or Fairbanks.

Whittier also swelled in population during this time, to its military high of 1,200 individuals. This was well below its emergency capacity of 30,000. A plan for possible emergency evacuation of Anchorage was kept in mind as the facility was being built, and a population of 30,000 in Whittier would be sustainable, though uncomfortable, for several days in the event of an emergency. Growth of Whittier was planned for, and many sections of land were left empty for future expansion.

A panoramic photo of Whittier and passage Canal from above in 1957 (below). Notice the tank farm and the two long docking berths jutting out into Passage Canal. None of these structures exist today, after the 1964 Earthquake.

If you compare the detail from the panorama (right) with the 1943 overhead photo on page 55, you can see the addition of the new Dock, on the left side of the photo, as well as quite a bit of filled-in land. of course the largest standout is the new 14-story Hodge Building at lower right. The Buckner building is visible, tucked into the forest in the upper right.

From Massive Plans to Meager Ends

Detail from above panorama, showing the Buckner Building, and the new dock facility (very long low building) below.

Second detail, showing the 14-story Hodge Building, several dozen temporary structures at right, and the tank farm and berths below. Whittier's present small boat harbor would be in the center of this photo if it were taken today.

Statehood, and Whittier's fast fade

The Korean War became a memory, and most of the major projects in Alaska had reached or approached completion. With momentum and support fading, the military presence in Alaska began to scale back. Construction crews and wartime personnel were the first to head back south. The established base at Whittier settled slowly into a routine of loading and unloading supply ships, passenger ships and trains. As time passed, the arriving supply ships became fewer and fewer, and the commercial ships began to far outnumber the military ships docking there. Whittier was transforming into a federally run commercial port, as the U.S. government owned

Another panoramic photo from 1957 (above), this time taken from across Passage Canal. Bard Peak is the massive tall mountain (3,517 ft.) at center. Hanging lazily above the townsite of Whittier is its namesake, the broad Whittier Glacier. On the right side of the photo, Portage pass can be plainly seen, with Portage Glacier barely visible in the background, nestled below Byron Peak

Below Portage pass (right) a few temporary and some permanent structures line the shore at the head of Passage Canal. The west tank farm, only just completed, would soon be pumping jet fuel to Elmendorf AFB in Anchorage.

and operated the port city as well as the railroad.

The Feds became deeply involved with Alaska in late 1958, as Congress finally signed into law a bill for Alaskan Statehood. President Eisenhower signed the bill on January 3, 1959, and the bustling territory became the 49th state of the United States.

Residents of Whittier, like a lot of Alaskans, were mostly happy about statehood, but with a few holdouts who would have rather remained independent. The celebrations raged statewide, despite any

Military tanks en route to Anchorage from Whittier in May of 1948. Thousands of tons of military equipment and supplies made their way to interior Alaska via this railway. (This photo formerly classified).

naysayers. Celebration faded in Whittier as the slowing of military trade came about. Seward was again competing heavily to be the port city for South Central Alaska and the government did not fight to keep shipping in Whittier.

Mothballed

Another restructuring of defense priorities and techniques led to a massive military reassessment again in the late 1950's. in September of 1960 Major General J.H. Michaels made a brief announcement in Anchorage that the entire port city of Whittier was to be inactivated. Due to "the steady decline in the amount of cargo, which has made the port uneconomical as an all-military port of entry." At this point in history, Whittier had handled over 2,000,000 tons of military supplies.

After 17 years as an active military port and only four years after the completion of its last large building, the city was to be mothballed. Only 800 people resided in Whittier in 1960 when the announcement came. Of the 800, only a skeletal maintenance crew of 48 was to remain.

The fate of the buildings and port was up in the air after this decision. The last ship loaded with military personnel left

Whittier's dock in October of 1960, only one month after inactivation. Military men like Col. E.H. Hauschultz, Chief of Army Transportation in Alaska, made up feasibility studies for Whittier. It was thought that the city might make an ideal industrial/commercial development, or perhaps an international resort destination. The massive concrete military structures would need to be made over into glamorous attractive hotels. It was seen as a potential winter destination, or a convention facility that could accommodate thousands.

The cost of the installation, including all buildings and facilities was estimated at $55,000,000 in 1960. The property was put up for sale or possibly lease, either in part or in whole. Private enterprisers and government bodies both showed interest, but stopped short of making concrete offers.

Unceremonious closure

Hard hit were the privately run businesses that had coexisted on the small plot of land with the Whittier complex. A lumber mill, creosote treatment plant, a Union Pacific petroleum tank farm, and a small fishing operation had established themselves over the last 17 years. The fishermen pulled out soon after the military had, as rail service slowed to a near-stop, with only an occasional maintenance trip from Whittier to Portage station, 14 miles distant. No roadway had ever been built, and direct train access to Anchorage ceased. The lumber mill, tank farm and treatment plant kept on, employing around 30 people.

After being mothballed, Whittier's facilities were maintained by a skeleton staff, to protect against the harsh climate.

In 1963 the Army officially ceased all activity in Whittier and began leasing the dock to the Alaska Railroad Corporation. The military maintenance crew of 30 was kept on, as the future of the complex remained uncertain. The ARR formed plans to expand operations in Whittier and began, slowly, to refit the railyard.

Life crept along at a snail's pace for the 65 residents of Whittier. In winter months, work and weather demanded constant attention. Relative boredom prevailed in the summer, with plenty of opportunity for leisure time fun, such as fishing and hiking. In January of 1964 the Koppers Company Creosote treatment plant shut down. After

In a scene not uncommon around Whittier, pilings from a long-ago abandoned dock at the head of Passage Canal lie tangled with driftwood.

The military had made such enormous plans for the region, only to walk away from most of them. Many structures built in support of those plans, or in hopes of them being completed lie strewn across the landscape in various states of disrepair or abandon.

A few of these wrecks are mixed together with rubble left over from the 1964 earthquake, occasionally surprising day hikers with miniature junkyards found in odd places.

just completing a large government order for railroad ties, it was underbid for a major project and folded up shop. Only ten men worked for Koppers Co., but the closure put 15% of Whittier's population out of work.

The harsh decline in Whittier's economy and population had ripple effects on neighboring communities such as Portage and Hope. Portage, a small town at the head of Turnagain Arm and on the opposite end of the rail spur from Whittier, was linked closely to Whittier and the Army base. Material moving to Whittier originated from or passed through the community surrounding Portage Station. Much of the lumber cut or processed in Whittier came from either Portage, or the small town of Hope, on Turnagain Arm's south shore. Hope's logging industry dove into a tailspin as the Army left and the Koppers Co. plant shut down.

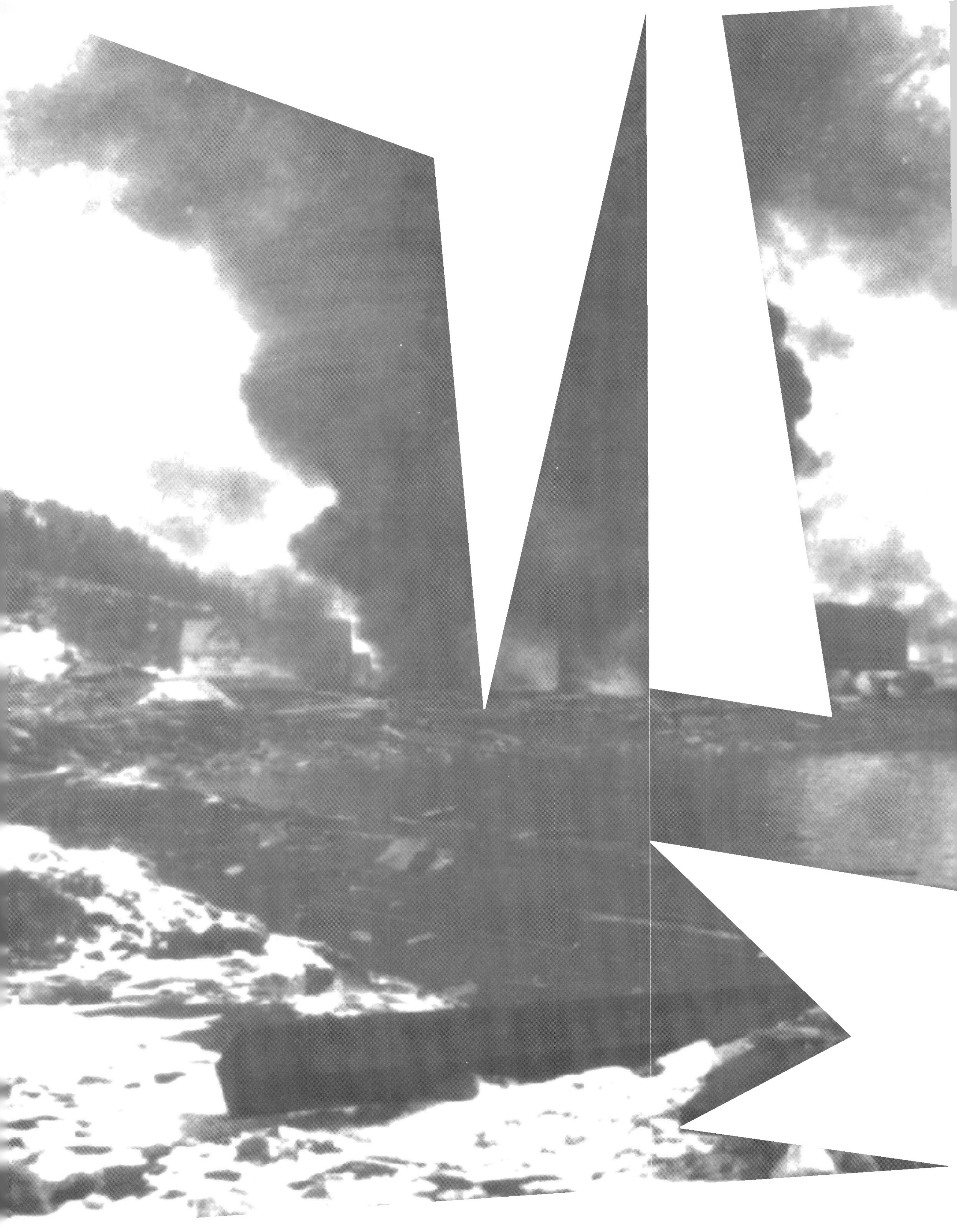

Chapter VI
The Quake and the Slow Road to Recovery

"Just when it looked like it couldn't get worse..."

March 27, 1964 was a Good Friday. Most of Whittier's 70 residents worked during that day. At 5:00 p.m. the cloud cover was gray and low, a light snow fell. The wind was calm and the water on Passage Canal looked glassy smooth. The Two Brothers Columbia Lumber Mill was changing shifts. The five men who worked for the Union Pacific Oil tank farm had the day off, some military maintenance workers remained on the large dock, a few people were preparing dinner in the small Whittier Manor, the Buckner and the Hodge. People moved about, heading home or finishing work shifts before a threatening heavy snow.

At 5:36 PM the shaking began. People on foot and inside were the first to feel it, the few on boats would feel it soon after. An earthquake was striking, its epicenter only 60 miles west of Whittier. The ground shook jarringly for those who were on bedrock. Those on loose soil felt a round-and-round motion. The violent shaking lasted for nearly four minutes.

Look at your watch and count out four minutes. Imagine the ground shaking so hard that you cannot even stand up for that entire time. This was the quake in Whittier.

The Buckner Building and Hodge Building swayed and moved. The eight-inch crumble joints between sections worked, as the separate sections banged loudly together, but stayed whole. On the 13th and 14th floor of the Hodge Building the metal plates that spanned the crumble joints were curled and bent by the violent

The largest buildings in Whittier are made up of multiple free-standing structures, separated by 8-inch gaps for earthquake safety. A metal plate crossing one of those gaps inside the Hodge building is seen here in 1964, bent by the force of the building segments smashing together.

The remains of the old Railcar Barge Slip Dock, March 1964. The lone, tilted tower used to be one of two towers that flanked the dock. Its twin tower sank into Passage Canal during the earthquake — its foundations torn away by underwater landslides. The slides, shaking, and subsequent tsunamis rendered this facility useless. Another new dock for offloading railcars was built soon after — using steel, not wood — just beyond the dock building visible at right.

motion, and some interior walls were cracked.

In Whittier the ground shook and settled 5.3 feet before it was over. On the shoreline, one tower of a rail-car barge dock swayed back and forth and collapsed onto the shore. The water of Passage Canal drew down just below it, as if the inlet were emptying into an enormous hole. Then the water rose, not violently, but in a glassy-smooth surge that rose 25 to 30 feet above sea level, flooding the waterfront with a swift tide.

As the first wave was beginning to flow back out to the Canal, the shaking began to slow and stop. The surface of Passage Canal became more and more disturbed, appearing to "boil out" in a massive surging area in the center of the inlet. The seawater from the expanding surge smashed ashore with more violence than the first wave, and was followed by a third, less violent, smaller wave. Two docks, each nearly a thousand feet long, were swept away. Pilings were ripped up and driven inland, becoming battering rams smashing into oil tanks and buildings.

The old tank farm in Whittier, ablaze on the shore of Passage Canal, March 27th — just after the earthquake. Torn open by the earthquake, the tanks spilled fuel oil, which ignited somehow soon after. Note the open water to the right of the burning tanks, where just minutes before two 1,000-foot long berthing docks had stood, stretching out into the inlet. Torn away by underwater landslides, they were then churned back onto the land, leaving pilings and planks strewn across the shore.

The sea halted its assault after three waves, leaving the townsite's shore in a shambles. The frightening noises of twisting metal, scraping concrete and rushing waters came to a stop. All of the Union Pacific Oil Company's petroleum tanks (more than a dozen) were damaged or destroyed, spilling thousands of gallons of petroleum onto the shore and into the Canal. A spark caught the spill and set it aflame. The shoreline burned with a thick black smoke rising above the waters.

The Two Brothers Columbia Lumber Mill buildings, shaken up, wave damaged and burned, turned into so much scrap lumber, and was abandoned. The small boat harbor and the two long docking berths used by Union Pacific had vanished into the sea. The car-barge dock was destroyed.

Of the 70 residents of Whittier caught in the great earthquake of '64, 13 died. They were all killed by the deadly waves that wrecked the shoreline. Of the 13, only one body was ever found, the rest, it is assumed, were swept far out to sea. Structural damage was estimated at $5,000,000.

Attending to the fires on land and caring for the few injuries, the 58 remaining citizens waited out the night in the dark, as the power plant had been damaged. Power was restored quickly though, and the lights were on by midnight.

The morning after

Saturday morning, March 28th, the morning scene appeared surreal. A light layer of snow still covered the surrounding mountains, smaller black plumes of smoke rose from the still-burning sea. The Buckner and Hodge Buildings survived whole with minimal damage, mostly to the Hodge's upper stories.

A reconnaissance airplane was heard buzzing through Portage Pass, and radio and visual contact was established. The few injured were picked up by helicopter

A close up look at the wreckage after the tank farm fire was extinguished. Earthquake, fire, water, and ice in a matter of hours — the damage was severe, as can be seen by the total loss evident in this photograph, taken eight days after the earthquake.

A photographer surveys the destruction on the Whittier waterfront, April 4, 1964. Notice the wave-like surface of the broken ground. After the earthquake, receding tsunami waters rushed back out to sea, toward the right side of the photograph, leaving behind these ripple-like patterns, ice and rubble.

later that same Saturday, and flown to Anchorage.

The earthquake had been measured at between 8.4 and 8.6 on the Richter scale, but was later officially revised to stand at a recorded 9.2 magnitude quake, the strongest ever recorded in North America. Statewide, 103 people lost their lives. Near Whittier, 31 people died in Valdez, 11 in Seward and 5 in Portage. Most of those deaths were caused by quake-related ocean waves. Eighteen people died in Anchorage, most in a severe landslide that destroyed a neighborhood that had been perched on a sea bluff.

Submarine landslides

The three sea waves that struck Whittier did not originate from the epicenter of the earthquake, or from further out to sea, as the Tsunamis in the movies do. These waves were local, and very damaging. As the rail-car barge dock's tower had collapsed, the ground beneath it was sliding away, downhill towards the sea floor in an underwater landslide. Another underwater slide occurred at the western end of Passage Canal.

As these landslides slid down, suction behind the slide drew the seawater down,

A stretch of the Seward Highway, near Portage Station, cracked wide open during the earthquake, as the silty ground beneath it gave way.

creating a hole, then it rebounded, filling the hole and washing ashore. Later, the mass of earth that slid away came to a rest at the bottom of the U-shaped canal, and the water that was being pushed forward by the slide pressed upward, causing the sea to boil up and out and crash ashore a second and third time.

Valdez and Seward both suffered similar wave destruction, though Valdez suffered more deeply. The seafloor of Port Valdez actually cracked open a fissure, draining seawater away. Then a large wave from Prince William Sound rushed in from further out, smashing ships far inland.

The railroad suffered minor damage in Whittier, some structural loosening of the small bridge over Whittier Creek, some misaligned rails, and a small amount of rockfall in the tunnels (which was cleared within two days). But just 14 miles distant, near Portage, the rails were twisted and flayed, bent into ribbons and junk.

Portage Valley lies based on a sandy silt that is hundreds of feet thick. When shaken in an earthquake, the water saturated silt becomes loose, soupy and unstable. Any solid objects on that ground move radically, sinking, twisting, or breaking apart. The earthquake's motion became amplified, as the vibrations rebounded within the valley. Imagine the loose silt surrounded by shaking mountains as jello in a shaking bowl — the jello still quivers long after the bowl has stopped. The shaking lasted a full 15 minutes in Portage, compared with four minutes in Whittier, only 14 miles away.

Portage was abandoned by its residents, and remains a ghost town today. The survivors who chose to stay moved to either nearby Girdwood or Anchorage. Girdwood's townsite was damaged by the settling of land and flooding caused by the earthquake, and the town moved uphill, further into Girdwood Valley. The same thing happened in Valdez, as the townsite was moved 7 miles west, to more solid ground. It pulled further away from the end of Valdez Arm, where damage should be less severe than 1964 when the next quake hits.

The bridge over Twentymile River collapsed during the quake, falling on its supports with such force that pilings punched right through the deck. This road and the railroad to the right were both damaged heavily, cutting off land transportation to Whittier for weeks.

The Quake and the Slow Road to Recovery

The ghostly remains of Portage, Alaska. The town was abandoned by its few residents after the earthquake. Rebuilding on unstable silty ground with a shaky local economy was too much to shoulder for those who had suffered through and survived.

Only a handful of buildings in various states of disrepair still remain, across the Seward Highway from the Portage Rail Station.

Seward was demolished by a powerful wave that tossed locomotives and fishing boats deep into town. The railroad was useless, roads were badly damaged, and airplanes and helicopters became the transportation of choice in Southcentral Alaska.

Getting back to business

The most populous part of Alaska, the South Central region, was without a functioning all-weather port. Realizing the need to get lifelines up and running quickly, the state of Alaska began work repairing the railroad first. The heaviest damage lay near the Twentymile River, close to Portage.

Rails were laid and bridges rebuilt swiftly in the warming spring weather. The Feds, who operated the Alaska Railroad, decided that damage had been lightest at Whittier, so repairs were initially concentrated there. A new rail-car barge slip was built and the first post-quake train rolled from Whittier to Anchorage on April 20th, 1964 — only 25 days after the 9.2 quake hit.

Commerce in Whittier picked up, but the population did not. The lumber mill was never rebuilt, the land it sat on had sunk more than 6 feet. The harbor lay useless, stripped of three out of its four docks. The only remaining residents were a handful of Army caretakers, railroad workers and Union Pacific workmen. Total population was somewhere around 40, varying weekly.

Restoration efforts in Seward took nearly

two years, rebuilding storehouses, docks, rails and trestles. In the first few years after the earthquake Whittier established itself as a major port once again. By 1967, Whittier was the busiest port facility in the whole state. Only five years previous, in 1962, Whittier's share of total Alaska cargo had been just 11 percent.

Whittier regains a population

A few workers began arriving over these years, rebuilding the tank farm, only now it was a government operation, and the tanks were rebuilt on more solid ground, further from the town. The tanks were also surrounded by protective earthen dikes to prevent any major spills in the future. The slowly growing population attracted a few others who could earn a living supporting the residents.

Control of the Port of Whittier was turned over to the U.S. General Services Administration (GSA) The property had been made available for limited leasing earlier, but with no real offers. Many plans had been drawn up for the port and now that it was a busy place once again, the GSA considered a proposal to sell the properties either piecemeal, or as a whole.

In 1967, a rebuilt version of the old West Tank Farm was completed, with an eight-inch pipeline connecting Whittier to distant Elmendorf Air Force Base in Anchorage. Petroleum could now be piped directly to the fuel tanks at Elmendorf without using any rail cars. The small pipeline runs parallel to the railroad tracks through a small tunnel of its own. It lays only inches below the ground's surface outside of the tunnels, and is made of a semi-flexible material, flexing rather than snapping in the next earthquake.

Plans were made to liven the prospects in the small town. Fishing operations returned slowly. Whittier's closeness to Anchorage by rail led to a number of boat owners from the big city keeping their boats anchored in Passage Canal, where they could be accessed easily. The next closest small boat harbor was Seward, 60-some miles to the south. Anchorage would never have a functional small boat harbor due to the shallow waters and high tidal fluctuations. The few vessels left in Anchorage harbors lie high and dry on the mud when the 35-foot tide is out.

Whittier becomes a city

Efforts to rebuild the old small boat harbor in Whittier were slow, the earthquake damage had been severe. The need was seen for a good harbor for both Whittier and Anchorage residents, and the citizens pushed the state government for assistance. For help with the harbor and other benefits, Whittier incorporated for the first time as a 4th class city in 1969 with a population of less than 70.

With help from the state, Whittier built an admirable modern harbor for $1.2 million. A harbor master was assigned and marine traffic was monitored by state officials and the U.S. Coast Guard. Expansions were made later to accommodate demand, and today's small boat harbor has more than 330 slips. Demand remains so high, mainly from boat owners in the Anchorage area, that slips are currently assigned on a waiting list system. How popular is it really? Well, the average wait is now over twelve years.

As Whittier had incorporated, officials were elected and town planning began. Among the first plans was the possible purchase of some or all of the buildings in town. Plans moved slowly though, and most efforts were quickly shelved. The state-run Alaska Marine Highway System constructed a dock in Whittier, and began ferry service in the early 1970's. The deals, signed by new officials of the City of Whittier, provided regular ferry links to Valdez and Cordova. Ferry service allowed a new freedom to those wishing to "get out of town", since the only other way was by private boat or rail.

In 1972 the State of Alaska eliminated the four-class system of town designations and replaced it with only two, first or second class. Whittier, as well as many other towns, enjoyed an automatic upgrade to a second-class city that year.

Whittier's small boat harbor today. Located right where the old tank farm used to stand. The harbor is very popular, and now has a 12-year waiting list for boat owners interested in a slip of their own.

Residents liked the town so much...they bought it

The earlier purchasing plans of city officials came back off the shelves and into heated discussion as a ballot issue. The citizens of Whittier were asked in a May election in 1973 to decide "should the City of Whittier issue $250,000 in general obligation bonds for the purchase of the 97 acre Military Facility, complete with structures?" The question involved every building maintained by the GSA and the Army, and all of the land platted by the military, save the tank farm.

The building formerly known as the Hodge. Residents of newly-founded Whittier renamed it the Begich tower in the 1970's, in honor of congressman Nick Begich, recently killed in a small plane crash. Nearly all of Whittier's residents live in this one 14-story building, with most others living in nearby Whittier Manor.

The measure passed by a vote of 66-13. The purchase was set into motion, and by August of '73, the GSA closed the deal with the City of Whittier, complete with a long-term lease agreement providing portions of the Hodge Building's first three floors for U.S. Army operations.

Later that same year the aging and vacant Buckner Building was dropped from the deal, and the purchase price was dropped to $200,000. The Buckner had been abandoned for over 10 years by then. Some basic maintenance had been performed to keep it presentable until the 1964 earthquake. Though not damaged by the quake, the Buckner did suffer some superficial problems. Cleanup efforts concentrated on the necessities and the buildings that were actually occupied, such as the Hodge. By the time of the purchase the Buckner was in such poor shape that it was assumed to be more of a liability than an asset for any who owned it. The GSA maintained ownership of the unwanted and vandalized Buckner. No real efforts were made to improve the site for a sale.

The city also exercised a privilege of ownership with their largest building, the Hodge. They renamed the Hodge as the Begich Tower, honoring of one of two congressmen killed in a plane crash in 1972. Nick Begich and Hale Boggs had been well-respected men and were honored throughout the state. Besides the Begich Tower in Whittier, on nearby Portage Lake, the U.S. Forest Service maintains a facility known as the Begich Boggs Visitor's Center in the shadow of Begich Peak.

Whittier began to grow in fits and spurts, but slowly. Talk went around of an unknown party trying to purchase the Buckner Building and convert it into a Casino. But the talk soon faded, generating little interest. There was more excitement in the early 1970's as the Alyeska Corporation had looked at Passage Canal as a potential terminus for its planned Trans-Alaska oil pipeline. For reasons of geography — no flat land near Whittier for a massive tank farm — and finances — the expense of shipping taxable oil through nearby Anchorage city borders and drilling new tunnels — Valdez was chosen over Whittier, Anchorage, or Cordova.

Imagine though, if Whittier had been chosen as the terminus city. It would have been likely that Exxon would have named their Supertanker the "Exxon Whittier" rather than the "Exxon Valdez." If that same spill had taken place, the resulting international media coverage would have made Whittier far more famous — or infamous— than it currently is.

The 800-mile long Trans-Alaska pipeline and Valdez terminal was completed and operational in 1977, but Supertankers weren't the only ships to be newly plying

A day boat heads away from Whittier, out Passage Canal towards Prince William Sound. Sightseeing cruises depart Whittier every day in the summer months for College Fjord, Columbia Glacier, Valdez, and more. Rail barges, professional fisherman, pleasure fishing expeditions, kayakers, and pleasure cruisers all use Whittier as home port.

the waters of Prince William Sound. Cruise ships began arriving in large numbers, adding new northern destinations to older routes that had traditionally sailed no further north than Glacier Bay.

Growth in the 1980's

Whittier gained a tourism industry. Charter fishing had long been popular and some sightseeing grew out of that. A few operators began giving local tours on large tour boats, sailing up College and Harriman Fjords, out into Prince William Sound and to Columbia Glacier and Valdez.

Cruise Ship arrivals added new money to city coffers as tourists passed through. But the amount of new money never proved vast, as most travelers just passed through Whittier in under an hour, sometimes within only a few minutes. The quick pass-through is due to a tight train schedule that keeps traffic moving along and a lack of major facilities for visiting tourists.

In the early 1980's, an Anchorage businessman named Pete Zamarello purchased the Buckner Building with a few grand ideas in mind. He decided that the former "City under one roof" would make an

The Buckner Building, left abandoned for much of its life, had fallen into terrible disrepair by the end of the 20th century. Aborted plans, financial troubles, and the increasing decay over the years all took their toll. Structurally, it is still sound, but superficially it has been in distress for years.

Evidence of the long time the Buckner Building has spent as a derelict - stalactites have formed on the ceilings all over the lower levels. Formed by rainwater seeping in for decades, limestone from the drywall on the floors above dissolves into the rainwater, then runs to the basement levels. The lowest level of the building can often be flooded with an influx of rainwater and groundwater.

excellent "Prison under one roof." After buying the property, Zamarello had much of it gutted, preparing for renovation. Only those fixtures bolted to the walls or floor were left behind. The gutting phase was as far as the project ever went, as Zamarello was unable to gain further developer backing for the project. One massive expense in the way of the attempted rehabilitation of the Buckner was safely removing the huge quantity of asbestos in the well-insulated building.

For various reasons Zamarello filed bankruptcy soon after, and the Buckner building, along with other holdings, became the property of numerous creditors of the estate. It has remained in limbo ever since, decaying and falling victim to vandalism, scavenging, and the punishment of Mother Nature. Nothing breakable inside the Buckner is left intact. All fixtures made of glass, porcelain, or wood have been smashed to pieces by vandals over the years.

Mixed tragedy on Good Friday

March 24, 1989 — a Good Friday. The Exxon Valdez oil Supertanker shored up on Bligh Reef, 70 miles due east of Whittier. Ineffective and slow response combined with a massive gash in the hull of the Valdez caused 11 million gallons of crude oil to spill unchecked into the waters of

Prince William Sound. 300,000 animals died, from sea otters to killer whales. Worst hit were the seabirds, ranging from puffins and bald eagles to ravens and seagulls.

To visualize the impact, note that a single quart of motor oil poured onto a body of water can cause a slick that covers nearly two acres. 11 million gallons of crude covered western Prince William Sound quickly, in 5 days the spill grew to over 50 miles in length. The oil splashed up on shorelines and islands, fouling water and land animals alike. The currents took the crude oil on a south-southwesterly path, missing Passage Canal and Whittier, but damaging nearby coastlines all along the Kenai Peninsula.

Response teams were formed in Valdez, Cordova, Whittier, Seward and Kodiak, totaling 10,000 individuals. The most fast and furious summer Alaska had seen since the Gold Rush then began. The populations of Alaska's towns normally swell in the summer months, as "snowbirds" return from their winter homes in Hawaii and California, and workers move north for the opening seasonal jobs. Most of the large projects in the state are completed in the summer. Oil work, road construction, tourism, fishing, timber, etc. are all nearly nonexistent during the cold months. Wages offered are high compared to similar positions out of state, designed to attract workers to commute north and offset the higher cost of living.

Exxon needed to assemble an army of thousands to assist with the cleanup efforts, and was forced to pay significantly higher wages than the going rate to attract so many so quickly. The result was a huge influx of cash into the small coastal towns near the spill site. Fishing boats and tour boats, whose normal runs were ruined by the spill, were chartered by Exxon for two, three, even up to ten times the going rate per day.

Whittier became a large center of cleanup activities and many of its citizens went to work, rescuing injured animals, scrubbing shorelines and rocks by hand and housing and transporting the thousands of workers. The task of feeding and supplying so many put the superstructure of Whittier under considerable pressure as well. As demand was high and people were very well-paid, rents and prices skyrocketed. Food and drink became as precious as gold.

It might seem to be an unfortunate paradox that such a disaster for the life and balance of Prince William Sound should have such a monetary benefit to those affected most. But consider that the flow of money stopped at the end of September 1989. Those who depend on the life of the sound have experienced years of hardship as the sea slowly heals itself.

As of this writing, most of Prince William Sound has recovered as far as it is able. Some of the beaches that were painstakingly cleaned rock by rock remain sterile places, having been cleaned of all life as well as oil. Some unscrubbed areas have been washed clean by natural tidal action over the years. Much of the leftover crude oil has either sunk or dissipated, some of it seeping into the beaches. Traces can still be found if one digs down 6 inches in a few

Regency Cruise Lines' Regent Sun, *docked in Whittier on an overcast morning in 1991. Disembarking passengers made their way to Anchorage next, either by bus, or by rail. Rail passengers would board passengers cars on the near side of the dock building in this photograph — the dark cars with white horizontal stripes.*

places. The Alyeska pipeline terminal continues its operations, and continues to experience small oil spills, which are inevitable.

Also, in another ironic twist, the attention focused on Prince William Sound during the spill and cleanup efforts increased interest and tourism to the area. The global media coverage of the spill acted as a phenomenal public relations campaign, attracting the curious and concerned. Cruise ship arrivals in Whittier began to pick up, as did more modern forms of tourism, such as kayaking and scuba diving.

Boatloads of tourists

The cruise ships arrived in Whittier's port at the end of their northbound journey, 1500-3000 passengers disembarking, with an equal amount arriving by train and bus to board the southbound ship. Although Whittier sometimes saw over 6,000 tourists pass through in a single day, the benefit to the town was often questionable. The passengers remain aboard the cruise ship while waiting for tour buses. They disembark, walk a few feet to board the bus, then ride onto the train — never spending more than a few minutes on the ground in Whittier. Lack of facilities available to tourists caused the tour companies to

> ### An Accidental Tourist
>
> Some visitors who arrive by sea are more than surprised to find themselves in Whittier. In 1998, a man who tried to take a nap in a railway boxcar in Canada found himself locked in and bound for Alaska with nothing to eat or drink.
>
> On arriving in Whittier, Alaskan police officer Dan Jewell found Tuan Quac Phan, 29, dehydrated, hungry and terrified after sailing to Alaska from Canada in the boxcar loaded on a barge, a trip that takes around five days.
>
> Tuan Quac Phan's accidental journey started in Prince Rupert, British Columbia, where, he said, he had climbed up in a boxcar to get out of the weather and to get some sleep.
>
> Officer Jewell was asked if Phan had anything to say, and he responded that Phan said only "Jail better. Jail better."

expedite travelers this way. The bulk of tour passengers never spend a dime in Whittier, but the ship's crew and staff and the bus drivers did spend their money. Drivers stayed overnight, and crew members wandered into the town for a break from life aboard the ships. If, however, a busload of tourists were to break down, 40 passengers became temporarily stranded. Whittier gift shops claim to have made more money from one broken-down bus than from a whole week of normal traffic.

To make up for costs of handling so many travelers, and to capitalize on the ship arrivals, the City of Whittier levied a $3.00 head tax on all cruise ship passengers in 1991. In response, all cruise lines except one abandoned Whittier in 1992. Five other cruise lines moved their end destination to nearby Seward, saving up to $9,000 per landing. The next year, 1993, no cruise ships arrived in Whittier at all.

A Princess Cruise Lines ship tied up at the Whittier dock in 1990. Cruise lines are monitoring recent developments with the new tunnel and road to Anchorage, and may soon return to Whittier as regular summer visitors.

Residents voiced

mixed reactions to the loss of the ships. Whittier's core population had reached a steady 275 year-round, swelling seasonally to 1,200 or 1,300 in the summer. Those who depended on the possible full train or broken-down bus reacted angrily, as a huge source of income evaporated. Those who had little to gain or lose from tourists welcomed the new quiet. No longer did they need to wait in long lines for the train or worry about thick black exhaust of some older cruise ships.

The head tax was lowered to $1.00 per person in 1995, and Regency Cruise Lines planned to return in the summer of 1996. Before any tours were booked though, Regency collapsed in bankruptcy in the fall of 1995.

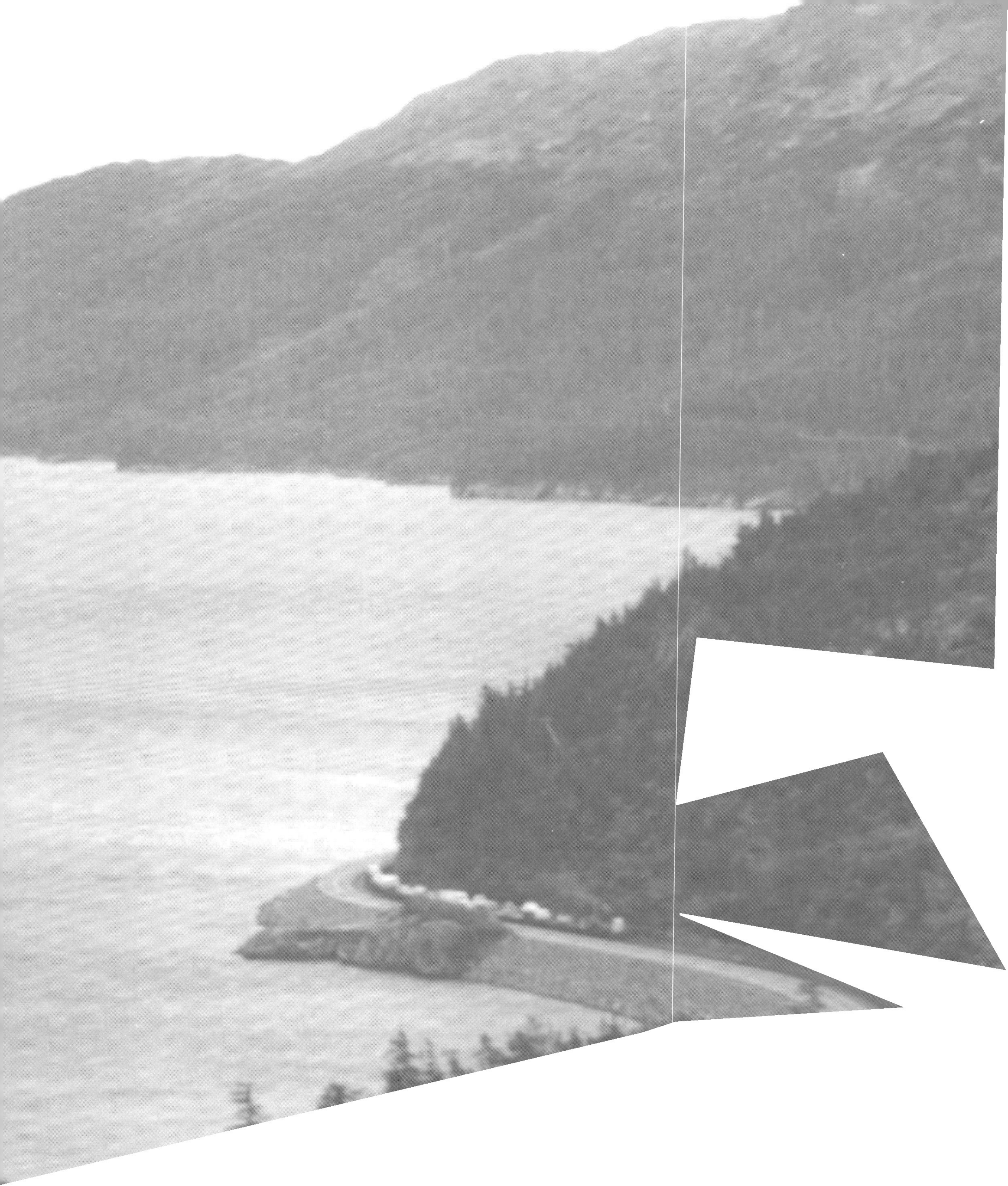

Chapter VII
Whittier Now

The Lay of the Land

Since humans first decided to use the Portage Valley as a thoroughfare between Prince William Sound and Cook Inlet, the ways they have traveled through it have changed drastically. Beginning with a relatively simple climb over the pass, becoming more dangerous over time — as the Portage Glacier receded, and ending with small aircraft, railroads, and now a shared-use road/rail tunnel.

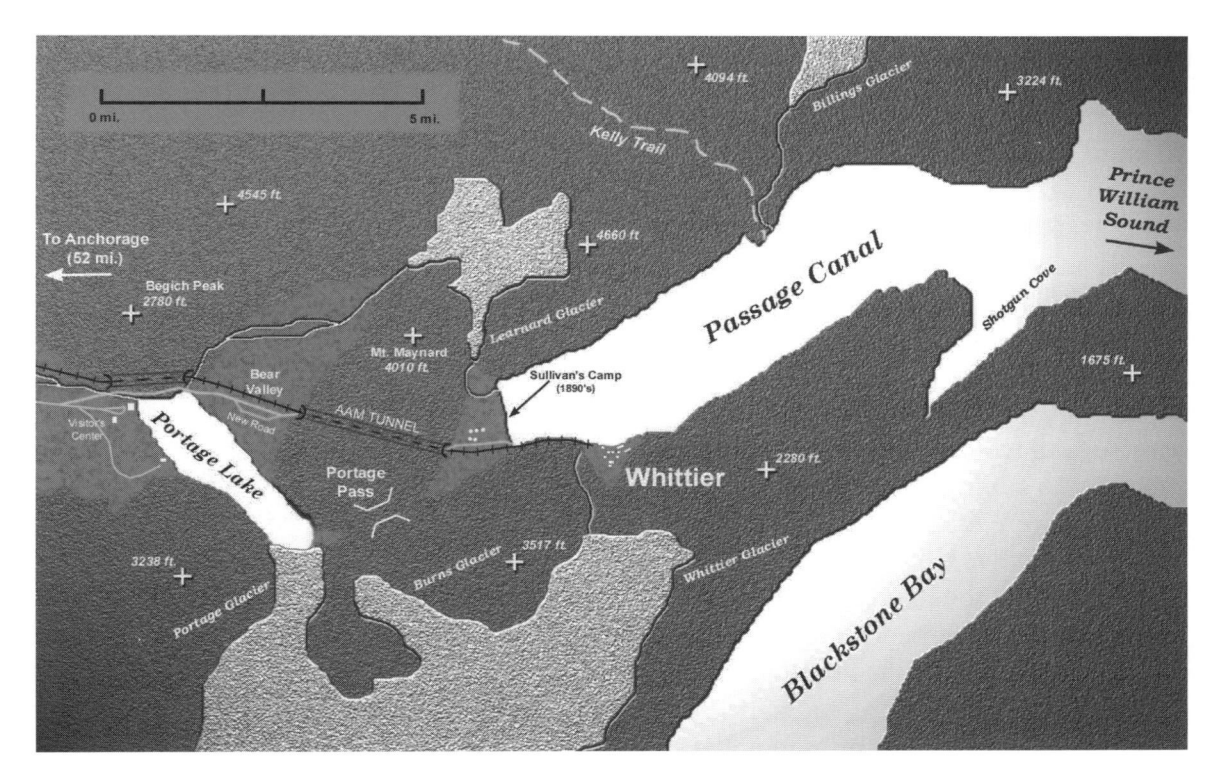

Whittier and its surrounding area. The triangle-shaped townsite of Whittier is at center, near the end of Passage Canal, a fjord branching off Prince William Sound. Nearly all of the land here is mountainous, with only a few relatively flat areas at the end of Passage Canal, in Bear Valley, and near Portage Lake. ("+" symbols mark mountain peaks).

The new road, existing railroad, tunnels and Portage Glacier Visitor's center are all located in the center left area. An unfinished pilot road exists heading eastward out of Whittier as well, towards Shotgun Cove, but dead-ends in a marshy field less than halfway there.

The Kelly Trail at top was named after a member of a military expedition in 1898. Kelly was searching for an easy land route to Knik Arm, on the northern side of Anchorage. He missed by a long shot, and ended up making a long, circuitous trip down Twentymile Valley to Turnagain Arm — only 18 miles west of where he began.

The continued efforts at preserving early trails, studying new ways through the area, digging the early tunnels, and now pushing through an $80 million road project all testify to the value of the region as a gateway. Prince William Sound is treasured, and most of those who treasure it come from the opposite side of Portage Valley.

The Road

Even before Whittier incorporated, plans to build a road out of town to connect to the Seward Highway were examined — going back to World War II. No fewer than 35 official studies have been made offering access alternatives since 1942. Proposed routes have included partial tunnels, graded climbs, and massive cuts. The road would replace the need for the Whittier shuttle rail service, and would open up the port to much more commerce. The first serious proposals were drawn up in 1978, including an alternative using an electric rail shuttle through the longer (Passage) tunnel. The '78 project disintegrated after an environmental impact had been completed. Another proposal was presented in 1984 at an estimated cost of $68 million dollars. The 1984 project was approved by the city with a vote of 85 to 14.

The federal government conducted a new survey to determine how best to build the access road and came up with three alternatives:

1. Drill entirely new tunnels parallel to the existing rail tunnels.
2. Pave and widen existing tunnels to accommodate both cars and trains.
3. Build a bridge near the Portage Glacier visitors center and pave only the longer tunnel.

The first option was abandoned as the cost of drilling entirely new tunnels would exceed $150 million dollars. The second option also was shelved, since it involved more new roadway to be built than the third option. The last plan, using the bridge, was adopted, but never got off the ground. The 1984 access project died in the state legislature after several studies.

Bond issues and road plans have been developed several times since then but until 1997, none proceeded further than the environmental impact reviews. 1991 estimates for the project ranged from $30 to $90 million dollars. Despite all attempts, the necessary approvals, funding and contracts had never lined up to produce results — until the most recent, the Whittier Access Project.

The Whittier Access Project received funding and approval as a part of a new initiative to further "open up Alaska" to recreation. The initiative, called "Trails and Recreational Access for Alaska", or TRAAK, was proposed and pushed through by Alaska's Governor, Tony Knowles. The decision was made to use the last of the three alternatives above, the Bridge-and-Toll-Road combination, to provide access to Whittier. Although this project was challenged, as others had been, it finally received approval in 1996 and is now completed. Key among the concerns expressed by some of those opposed to the road were the new construction on Federal lands, which were supposed to be set aside and untouched (part of the new roadway runs through federal park lands). However the Environmental Protection Agency and a federal judge gave their final approval and the tasks were opened up to bids.

Several construction companies began work over the Spring and Summer of 1997, overseen by the Alaska Department of Transportation.

The resulting road system is unique in the world — an $80 million 2.6-mile-long shared-use car-train toll road. It is also the first toll road in the state of Alaska. As of January 2000, the cost-per-vehicle for the toll road was still undecided, though it was estimated at $15.00 to $20.00, probably more for buses. The tolls are for round-trips, and are charged to drivers as they enter Whittier — there is no charge on the

---

Construction planned/completed for the new road

— A new two-lane bridge over Portage Creek leading from the existing road by the Portage Glacier Visitor's center.
— A new 430 foot tunnel drilled through part of Begich Peak, on the west side of Bear Valley.
— Cuts in the shoulder of Begich Peak just above the surface of Portage Lake.
— A new bridge over Placer Creek in Bear Valley.
— A scenic turnout near Placer Creek.
— A two-lane roadway through Bear Valley and a large "staging area" for over 400 cars to wait for the long drive through the 2.6 mile long Anton Anderson Memorial (AAM) Tunnel.
— Toll-collection facilities (to cover the costs of construction and maintenance).
— Removal of existing railroad tracks and ties in the AAM tunnel.
— Placement of "modules" in place of the old railroad track. The modules are 7-foot wide concrete pads with two slots in them to accommodate rails. Lined up end-to end, they form a flat roadway for cars with rails right down the middle for trains.
— Scraping and excavating the AAM Tunnel interior in places for ground support systems, ventilation, drainage, safe "pull-out" areas for cars, and a bit of extra clearance for new "double-stack" trains (two containers stacked on top of each other on a rail car).
— Building 8 "safe houses" for shelter inside the tunnel at 1,600-foot intervals, each will be about 32-by-36 feet, large enough for 55 people, with independent water, air and restrooms.
— Installation of safety and support systems, including ventilation, fire suppression and lighting. Ventilation along the tunnel ceiling includes six 75-horsepower jet fans (which look like small airplane jets) for normal operation and four 300-horsepower normal fans for emergencies.
— Traffic monitoring systems, such as magnetic sensors and video cameras, and communications systems to coordinate traffic. (They need to be sure that if 12 cars go in one end, that all 12 come out the other end!)
— A second staging area on the Whittier side of the AAM Tunnel.
— A short connecting road to the (small, but existent) Whittier road system.
— Overall improvements to Whittier's system of bridges and roads
— A public Rest Area and Bathroom facility in Whittier.

return trip.

In the long battle over road access, there have always been supporters and detractors. Supporters of the road have included the majority of residents of Whittier, residents of nearby Girdwood — who would benefit from increased traffic, residents of Anchorage who desire easier access to tidewater recreation, freight transport companies who could use Whittier's docks to load trucks directly, and surprisingly, the Alaska Railroad.

The ARR Whittier shuttle's earnings from passengers, freight and tour buses were high in summer months, high enough to make some suspect ARR of milking a captive public. 1994 one-way ticket prices ranged from $13.00 for a single walk-on to $535.00 for a truck over 60 feet long. However, lower rates were charged in the balancing 7 winter months, and despite fewer runs per week (four), the shuttle ran at a deficit all winter, struggling to fund service and maintenance. The total earnings, averaged over the year lined up in the negative columns of the ARR ledger, the shuttle was a money loser.

Residents of Whittier may or may not be excited about the new road, and the open access to the world, but they are definitely apprehensive about a few things. For one, owning a car in Whittier used to be a necessity — leaving town meant a train trip plus a 50 mile drive. Now, owning a car in Whittier may be a liability if the huge estimated crowds arrive. Parking and getting around may become difficult - Whittier may experience a whole new kind of traffic jam. Another issue is that of preparedness. Are there enough facilities to accommodate the predicted onslaught of new visitors? (The State estimates 1.4 million visitors annually, up from a current level of 220,000). The answer is no, there aren't enough facilities now, and the State of Alaska has indicated it may help out with construction if necessary. Long and short-term parking facilities, housing, dining and public facilities may become scarce, and neither the City nor the State have done much to prepare. Additionally, unless visitors are headed out to Prince William Sound on a tour or fishing boat, there is not much "in town" for visitors to do at all.

On the flip side of that coin, if the hordes of anticipated new visitors fail to arrive — if the toll is too high, or the tunnel traffic coordination too difficult, or if they "just don't come" — those who speculated, or are counting on the extra revenue may find themselves caught short, and few are willing to take such a risk.

Major concrete benefits the road brings include increased accessibility to local communities, meaning you don't have to live in Whittier to work there - you can easily commute from Girdwood or elsewhere. Also, convenience of access for residents, no longer do they have to rely completely on a rail schedule. Trips to Anchorage only involve a wait at a staging area at worst now — no fears of full trains in the summer months or the trouble of too few trains running in the winter.

One interesting result of the road being

built is the uncertain future of the rail station in Portage — the gravel parking lot and ticket booth off the Seward highway that used to be the "other end" of the Whittier Shuttle's run. Nobody seems to know what the future of rail passenger traffic to Whittier will be, and whether the Portage Station will be mothballed or changed to some other sort of facility. Only time will tell.

Whittier today

As of 1999, Whittier has built up over 70 local businesses, nearly half being operated by outside interests. The Begich Tower was incorporated as the BTI, or Begich Tower, Inc. Condominiums. The city operates with an annual budget of $650,000. Much of the population works for the Alaska Railroad. For a time recently, the man who took your tickets o the train was also the Mayor of Whittier. Despite the coming of the road, rail traffic is expected to increase with more freight, so those with ARR jobs appear to be secure despite the elimination of the Portage Shuttle.

In 1993 and 1994 the City of Whittier gained an additional 600 acres of land along the south shore of Passage Canal. This property was granted to the city by the state of Alaska in 1984 with the provision that all land not needed for expansion or public use be sold within ten years.

The additional land is situated around two coves, Emerald Cove and larger Shotgun Cove. Prospective landowners would have to travel 3 or 4 miles east of town to visit their sites. City planners started a primitive road to Shotgun Cove earlier, in 1984. The road still exists, more a rough path than a drivable road now, and ends in a remote boggy marsh, where

A typically multi-purpose Whittier institution, the Anchor Inn — halfway between the Begich Tower and the shoreline — is a hotel, a restaurant, a bar, a grocery store, a laundromat, and even has several condominiums.

Frigid temperatures freeze the surface of Whitier's small boat harbor in this photograph. Many boats are hauled out during winter months. Those still in the water must be watched closely, as heavy snow buildup can easily sink an unattended vessel.

builders ran out of money. Most interested parties use boats to access Shotgun Cove, landing on the shore and wading a little, rather than hiking miles through dense brush.

After an initial flurry of interest in the finalized acquisition, the problem of what to do with the property remains up in the air. The city retains a number of choices, including development for recreational purposes, opening access and creating a Whittier suburb, or leaving the land open — retaining it for the value of the property. Development plans have been presented for the acreage which triples the size of Whittier, but no direct actions are being taken.

Current life in Whittier depends heavily on the season, much as it does all over the North. Spring and summer bring economic booms of tourism, construction, fisheries, and boating activity. Early fall closes the fishing season with a large run of silver salmon. Winter settling in brings snow, cold and darkness — even when the winter sun shines Whittier is in shadow, located in a deep valley.

At the beginning of the 21st Century, millions of dollars had been committed by state and federal government agencies toward the upgrading and rebuilding of various parts of the city. Crumbling docks will be refurbished, visitor facilities will be built, and a much-needed pedestrian overpass will be built connecting the residential area to the waterfront, crossing over the dangerous railyard below. Hundreds of thousands of dollars are targeted toward upgrading the rail facilities as well. In 1998 nearly 7,000 rail cars arrived in Whittier via barge,

The Portage Shuttle (above). Run by the Alaska Railroad, the shuttle was the only land-based way into Whittier for decades. Passengers could either ride on a passenger-only rail car, or they could drive right onto the backs of flatbed rail cars (below) and spend the 12-mile journey in their cars, carried along by the train. While the journey was certainly unique, it was never convenient, and could be very costly. The new toll road changes everything, and the fate of future passenger rail service to Whittier remains unknown.

The first arrival of a railcar barge, also known as a Hydro-Train, into Whittier's new slip dock in the 1950s. This dock and the two berths in the background were demolished in the 1964 earthquake.

headed inland to Anchorage and Fairbanks. With a widened new tunnel, the Alaska Railroad expects to increase that traffic even more.

Before the road was built, if you missed the last train out of town on a given day, you became a "POW", or Prisoner of Whittier. After the final train, no other options were available, save a long hike or a very, very long boat trip. Overnight accommodations are available at the Anchor Inn or the Sportsmen's Inn (approximately 40 beds) for travelers awaiting the next trip in the morning (or perhaps several days later!).

A rolling railcar ramp. This strange contraption is used to offload rail cars from double-deck barges. Cars from the lower deck roll right onto rails on the ground. Cars from the upper deck are lowered gingerly down this ramp to the switching yard below.

A railcar barge in dock in 1998. This new slip dock was built 250 feet east of the old one after the '64 quake. Heavy duty tug boats pull these barges through the Gulf of Alaska from Vancouver, B.C. and Seattle, WA.

Life in isolation

A typical "run to town" to Anchorage used to be an expensive undertaking before the road was completed. A round-trip rail ticket for a vehicle with 2 occupants ran $70 dollars. Added to that the cost of gasoline for a 100-mile round-trip from Portage station to Anchorage and back, plus the cost of whatever goods you went to town to buy. The "trip to town" could have easily run over $100 dollars. Since the road was built, the cost is slightly less, but the level of convenience has gone way up.

Whittier can be a very confining place to live, and there are numerous stories to be found of individuals who never leave their apartment for years at a time. Oddly, there are even those who compete for bragging rights, seeing how long they can go without leaving their condo or building. Groceries are delivered or brought by friends, and trash is left in the hall or taken out by friends or neighbors. Even active people find they rarely leave the condos of the BTI, and need to make a conscious effort to leave town completely.

The infrastructure of stores, school and housing is so close and efficient, the need to go outside rarely arises. Back when it was a purely military facility, a story circulated regarding several young men who arrived as soldiers on a transport one day, entered one of the interconnected buildings, and never set foot outside again

The Whittier Manor and Sportsmen's Inn Bar and Cafe. Most residents of Whittier who do not live in the Begich Tower call the 80-unit Whittier Manor home.

until several years later, as they departed at the end of their tour of duty.

Bring on the cable TV

Just as electricity was difficult to bring to the construction site in the 1940's, cable television proved difficult to be had in the 1980's, and regular television reception was nonexistent because of the high mountains all around. But one day former city mayor Kay Shepard discovered a loophole in a state funding process. Shepard was able to take advantage of this and provide cable to the entire town. It seems that municipally affiliated non-profit organizations are eligible for state funds for certain civic projects. Kay Shepard established the non-profit Whittier Museum in an empty room on the ground floor of the BTI, and was able to have the state of Alaska fund most of the cost of running a cable TV access line to the museum for "educational" purposes. With the establishment of the access line, the entire town was soon able to plug in and enjoy access like any number of big city homeowners. Only a few radio stations are available via translator stations from Valdez and Anchorage.

Activity in Passage Canal

Commerce revolves around the train. Sealaska Corporation operates two-level sea barges that carry railcars between Whittier and other Pacific ports, primarily Vancouver, B.C. and Seattle, WA. Barges arrive around three to five times per week. Rail cars are offloaded into the Whittier yards and trains are "built" one car at a time, then pulled north to Anchorage or Fairbanks. An oil barge used to arrive once a week to fill the oil tanks on the western shore with petroleum for Elmendorf Air Force Base. The tanks are in disuse now, and the Government is exploring ways to clean up and open up the land for future use.

Once a week a doctor visits the local clinic. A Physician's Assistant is on call seven days a week, but all medical emer-

The Strangest Town in Alaska

gencies are helicoptered to Anchorage. Some maintenance of the small boat harbor is necessary in the winter. Snow loads become so heavy that boats can sink under the weight, so snow must be shoveled as needed. The single liquor store is open all day, six days a week in the summer, but opens only three hours a day in the colder months and surprisingly, sales plummet. A videotape rental facility and tanning booth parlor are located in the same room, in the BTI, down the hall from the museum. Two bars and restaurants are open in the winter. A knot of gift shops, restaurants and snack bars crowd together in a small area known as "the triangle", on the waterfront near the tour boat passenger docks.

Recreation comes in all forms. Whittier is known as a "gateway to Prince William Sound", and is the jumping-off point for a large number of excursions. Summer activities include hiking, camping, fishing, hunting, kayaking, pleasure boating, sightseeing and rock climbing. Winter brings out cross-country skiing, snow machines, ice climbing and snowman competitions. Whittier is a base for southcentral Alaska scuba diving activity year-round. It is one of the few available locations for Alaskan divers to become certified in the winter.

Daily life is much the same as in any small American town. Often slow-paced and quiet on the surface, but teeming below. Everyone knows everyone else's business. Political differences become personal conflict in the blink of an eye. The close quarters of the BTI and the Whittier Manor keep the gossip mills well-fed. Crime is nearly non-existent, save for petty

Whittier's school, located behind the Begich Tower. Classes are available for younger children, with older children boarding in Anchorage for their high school years.

An unsubstantiated story

Back in the late 1980's, a gentleman from Anchorage, who had been out of work for some time applied for a temporary position in Whittier that would pay very well. The day of his interview arrived and he found himself leaving Anchorage very late — the interview was in Whittier, 50 miles and a train ride away. Speeding all the way to the train station in his small truck, the gentleman arrived excitedly only to find out he had just missed the train. He had only 20 minutes to get to Whittier, or he'd miss the interview. and no way of getting there.

Bravely (or desperately, (or stupidly)), he sped off from the ticket office, drove up the embankment, and took off bouncing down the railroad track — his right-side tires in between the tracks, his left-side tires along the outside. 12 miles of punishing railroad ties was too much for his small pickup to handle, he only made it about four miles back — not even to the first tunnel — before a tire blew out.

The track at this point was on a raised ridge — marsh water to either side of it. With no way to get off the track and nowhere to go even if he could get off, the gentleman started walking back to the rail station — having given up hope for the interview.

Well, the train he had missed soon emerged from the tunnels on its return trip to find a little yellow pickup abandoned on the tracks ahead. Slowing and sounding the horn, the engineer couldn't see anyone who belonged to the truck.

On a tight schedule and running late, the engineer made an executive decision, and slowly pressed forward — indelicately pushing the pickup forward, then off to the side and into the marsh.

By the time the authorities and Railroad people had finished with him, our job seeker found himself in a situation far worse than before.

He was fined by the State Troopers for trespassing and damaging property, the Alaska Railroad sued for damages to the locomotive and the tracks caused by the violent shoving aside of the truck, the EPA fined him for spillage of oil and gasoline when his truck sank in the marsh, he had to pay for the crane to be brought in to recover the truck, and the tow truck to return it 50 miles to Anchorage, the truck was totaled (and he was uninsured), and he didn't get the job he so desperately wanted.

Someone made an estimate that it would have been far cheaper — in hindsight — if he would have driven to nearby Girdwood and chartered a helicopter, rather than trying to drive down those rails.

---

vandalism, a few drug problems, and the occasional bar brawl. The small school is located behind the BTI and is connected to it by another tunnel. It houses five classrooms with five teachers, with a student body ranging from 30 to 50 children, kindergarten through eighth grade. High school students are sent off to Anchorage and boarded while they attend public school.

"Why would you want to live there?"

The reasons for moving to Whittier are as diverse as the population, from a love of seclusion to a result of circumstances. Those who stay do so by choice, rarely by default. A few who had served in the military in Whittier at one time have

Summer months bring hikers to the Chugach Mountains. This photograph was taken from the top of Portage Pass, looking down toward Passage Canal. The railroad and west tank farm can be seen in the center. Although the pass no longer connects Whittier to the Portage Valley directly, the hike is still beautiful, relatively simple and rewarding.

chosen to return and call it home. Rents used to be inexpensive, averaging around $300 per month for a one-bedroom condo in 1995. Prices have risen however, and now can reach $900 per month for some of the better apartments. The location is enticing in its own way, remote and beautiful, surrounded by mountains, glaciers and the sea.

Most residents are proud of their town, and defend it as the most beautiful place in Alaska. Yet others deride it as a boring desolate scrapyard of a community, and

The view from the top on the other side of Portage Pass. Portage Glacier snakes its way down to the surface of Portage Lake. The body of water in the foreground is only a small pond at the top of the pass.

The dark section in the middle of the face of the glacier is surface rock only recently exposed by the fast-receding glacier. Former estimates stated that the Glacier would pull out of the lake in 2020, but it beat that time by nearly 20 years.

Hiking forward, toward the glacier, the Pass Trail ends at the shores of Portage Lake.

Although travelers could walk its surface like a highway less than 100 years ago, access to the glacier itself is now cut off by the lake and a large stream flowing from Burns Glacier, just out of the photo to the left.

refer to an old phrase that goes "if God had to give the world an enema, he'd stick the hose in Whittier." The latter sentiment is most often uttered during one of Whittier's dismal weather swings.

Rumors abound

Diversity of opinion has resulted in many disparities, including historical problems. In researching this book, the author ran across many conflicting stories and figures relating to Whittier's past. Rumors abound where facts are fuzzy. Historical records on Whittier are few and some coverage is hazy at best.

Rumors overheard include the notion that the Buckner Building has not only six stories above ground, but houses 11 levels of basements. It is unknown how this rumor started, but it is quite improbable, since 11 stories down would be far below sea level, only a few hundred feet from shore.

Another obscure one involves a supposed massive military project planned to create a secret submarine base. The base was to have been housed in Portage Lake, removed from seawater, and probably overlooked by enemy reconnaissance photographs. An underwater underground tunnel would be drilled through the isthmus, deep below the rail tunnels. The tunnel would connect the seawater of Passage Canal with the glacial Portage Lake. It is not known if that project would even be possible to complete today, but the cost of such a task would be phenomenal.

Still another set of historical rumors involve the 1964 earthquake, saying that a large tsunami roared in from Prince William Sound and splashed up to the 10th floor of the Begich Tower. Also that 30, not 13 people were killed, and that Whittier was cut off from the world for 3 weeks as smoke, flames and quake damage kept any rescuers from arriving. Though more dramatic and dynamic than the truth, none of the above actually happened. Three sizable waves, caused locally, took 13 lives. No floodwater reached the Begich Tower, and rescues were performed the very next day by helicopter.

Lastly, but certainly not least, is the weather. The author has read annual precipitation figures for Whittier of 148, 170, 174 and 188 inches. It's probably closer to 174 inches (14.8 feet!). Annual snowfall has been listed at 210, 260, 280 and 510 inches. Again, probably closer to 260 inches (nearly 22 feet.) Twelve inches of snow = one inch of rain. The heaviest snowfall on record was 47 feet during a harsh, wet winter all over Alaska. Suffice to say that Whittier is an extremely wet place.

Entering the 21st Century

Whittier has enjoyed a stable existence in the recent past in contrast to its historical ebb and flow. The impact of the new access highway will change the character of the town completely. The 1.4 million annual visitors eventually brought in by the new road will likely affect every aspect of life

An Alaska Railroad train carrying cars, trucks and trailers makes the easy curve along Passage Canal, headed toward Portage Station.

for residents, many of whom have said they'd move away when the road is completed, and some of whom already have moved on. The road will also likely infuse the population with newcomers and drive an expansion of the economy and the housing market. Some growth seems inevitable, with phenomenal growth possibly following.

Business interests, both local and from outside Whittier, are throwing their weight behind the momentum building around the opening of the new road. Cruise ship companies are being wooed to return to the town, private facilities to house boats and vehicles are being planned, more retail facilities are being planned, and of course, much more parking is being developed. If the city can lure the cruise ships back from Seward, the benefit is not only for the owners of the docking facility, but also for local business. Even if the bulk of tourists pass straight through town on the way to Anchorage, crew members, bus drivers, and the occasional tourist will still be arriving in town, often just looking for a place to eat, get a cup of coffee, or buy some gifts.

As demand has grown, so have property values. Since most folks in Whittier live in the Begich Tower, it can be viewed as a small community unto itself. Apartments in the Tower that sold for $10,000 in 1994 were selling for $35,000 to $60,000 in 1999. Any land left available for sale at the end of 1999 was seen as more expensive than just the cost of the land itself, because it was entirely undeveloped — with no immediate access to power, sewer, phone ar any other utilities. The cost of bringing those facilities even a short distance is very high, but as soon as one development brings it in, others will follow as the cost goes down.

The Shotgun Cove development has the potential for huge success as a recreational or residential area, and may prove to be the star in Whittier's crown yet. The future of the vacant Buckner Building remains up in the air, its deterioration accelerating daily. The building has been acquired by a consortium of Anchorage businessmen in 1998. Called the Prince William Resort Corporation, they have expressed interest in refurbishing the structure into a world-class resort and condominium complex, but so far they have not publicly gone further than stating their intentions to build. Before that, the last known serious inquiry into acquiring it was the Baptist Church in the early 1990's. They had looked into it as a possible retreat and worship facility. A second small boat harbor lies in the possible future, as does a new development along the shoreline.

Life still goes on now as it has for years before, citizens living in one of two buildings, protected from nature and the outside world, dealing with the new road and all the changes associated with it.

As long as Whittier has had a population, it has been a small town often immersed in slow-moving massive projects.

Billings Glacier, seen across Passage Canal from Whittier. Once, when plans were afoot to convert the Buckner Building into a new prison facility for Alaska, some wags remarked that it wouldn't be very punishing — since prisoners would have views like this from their cell windows. The plans for the prison fell through, but the views are still there for anyone to take in.

From the building of the first wooden military town, to the construction of the two largest buildings in Alaska at the time, to the recovery efforts after the '64 quake, to the building of the new road and all the new facilities it will require — when a new project begins, it always has a massive scale. Hemmed in by 4,000 foot tall mountains, most of Whittier's living space and access paths have been blasted out of solid rock, at much cost and work. Those who built the town were determined to finish the arduous task, and those who moved there and lived there were equally determined to have a new life, one of isolation in a beautiful but harsh corner of Alaska. The arrival of the new road means change, in some cases monumental change for a small town of 300 people. As Whittier steps into the 21st century, it now has new connections to the outside world, and is now capable of keeping up with the rest of Alaska, moving at a brisk pace with more options, rather than remaining deliberately isolated. There are those who treasured that isolation, but for better or worse, the old "can't-get-there-from-here" town of Whittier is now a thing of the past — left back in the 20th century.

About the Author:

   Author and publisher Alan Taylor spent the better part of five years working in South Central Alaska in the tourism industry, primarily based in Anchorage and Valdez. Alan currently works and lives in Seattle, Washington, with his wife Christina, and tries to return to Alaska as often as possible, (though never often enough!)